Enacting Self-Study

in Education

Shirley R. Steinberg
General Editor

The Counterpoints Primers series is part of the Peter Lang Education list.
Every volume is peer reviewed and meets
the highest quality standards for content and production.

PETER LANG
New York • Berlin • Brussels • Lausanne • Oxford

Derek Markides

Enacting Self-Study

Learning and Leading Through Love

PETER LANG
New York • Berlin • Brussels • Lausanne • Oxford

Library of Congress Cataloging-in-Publication Data

Names: Markides, Derek, author.
Title: Enacting self-study: learning and leading through love /
Derek Markides.
Description: New York: Peter Lang, 2022.
Series: Counterpoints primers; vol. 38 | ISSN 2572-5831
Includes bibliographical references.
Identifiers: LCCN 2022016506 (print) | LCCN 2022016507 (ebook)
ISBN 978-1-4331-9689-8 (paperback)
ISBN 978-1-4331-9592-1 (ebook pdf) | ISBN 978-1-4331-9593-8 (epub)
Subjects: LCSH: Educational leadership. | Self-consciousness (Awareness) |
Educators—Conduct of life.
Classification: LCC LB2806. M3675 2022 (print) | LCC LB2806 (ebook) |
DDC 371.2—dc23/eng/20220617
LC record available at https://lccn.loc.gov/2022016506
LC ebook record available at https://lccn.loc.gov/2022016507
DOI 10.3726/b19700

Bibliographic information published by **Die Deutsche Nationalbibliothek.**
Die Deutsche Nationalbibliothek lists this publication in the "Deutsche
Nationalbibliografie"; detailed bibliographic data are available
on the Internet at http://dnb.d-nb.de/.

Cover design by Clear Point Designs

© 2022 Peter Lang Publishing, Inc., New York
80 Broad Street, 5th floor, New York, NY 10004
www.peterlang.com

All rights reserved.
Reprint or reproduction, even partially, in all forms such as microfilm,
xerography, microfiche, microcard, and offset strictly prohibited.

CONTENTS

Tables	vii
Acknowledgments	ix
Introduction	1
Chapter 1 Self-Study and Autobiography	3
Chapter 2 Self-Study and Literature	39
Chapter 3 Enacting Self-Study	71
Chapter 4 A Critical Personal History Self-Study	91
Chapter 5 How Do I Continue? Given What I Understand.	123
Glossary	129
References	135

TABLES

Table 1. Shifts in Educational Leadership Through Time as Adapted from Bedard and Mombourquette (2015) — 43

Table 2. Findings (actions required) and Recommendations (for increasing adaptive learning capacity) of and for Effective High School Redesign Implementation as Adapted from Friesen et al. (2015) — 45

Table 3. Prominent Metaphors and Associated Affordances Adapted from Gereluk et al. (2016); Entailments Related to Metaphors (Davis & Renert, 2013a, 2013b) — 51

Table 4. Five Foci Framework for Self-study, Adapted from Samaras (2011, pp. 72-73) — 78

Table 5. Determinants of Relational Trust and Indicators as Adapted from Robinson (2011) — 87

Table 6. Suggestions to Increase Validity in Self-Study as Adapted from Feldman (2003, pp. 27-28) — 88

Table 7. Binaries Associated with Some Leadership Characteristics by Category as Adapted from Hutchins and Storm (2019) — 116

Table 8. Logic of Life Descriptors and Characteristics as Adapted from Hutchins and Storm (2019) — 117

Table 9. Shifts From Past Logic Towards a Regenerative Leadership/Logic of Life as Adapted from Hutchins and Storm (2019) — 118

ACKNOWLEDGMENTS

To Jennifer, my trusted one, my heart. Ashwin and Evren, my catalysts for envisioning divergent educational possibilities.

Thank you to Dr. Shirley Steinberg, my mentor and supporter for guiding me throughout the writing process, and to Dr. Brent Davis for guiding me towards the language of complexity.

Finally, to my critical friends, I am indebted and grateful.

This book was originally written as my doctoral thesis and portions of the dissertation have been subsequently published as journal articles. Parts of the sections specifically focusing on educational leadership were published in the International Journal of Leadership in Learning, and sections focusing on the the emergent themes and pedagogies of love were published in Research in Educational Policy and Management. I am indebted to both journals and the editors for their support. The portions that exist in this book were reproduced with their permissions.

INTRODUCTION

To understand education, one must love it or care deeply about learning, and accept it as a legitimate process for growth and change. To accept education as it is, however, is to betray it. To accept education without betraying it, you must love it for those values that show what it might become. (Battiste, 2013, p. 190)

Engaging in a bricolage of critical personal history self-study allowed one school administrator to better understand his roles, responsibilities, and formation of identity within the context of a school system while envisioning the divergent possibilities of a yet-to-be-known future through the lens of love. Pedagogies of love can be understood as more than the embodiment of romantic notions of the word. Pedagogies of love enact relationality: blending care, commitment, knowledge, responsibility, respect, and trust (hooks, 2001). Ever-evolving and situational, these pedagogies are understood as tentative. During the self-study process (Samaras, 2011), affective experiences were reflexively interrogated to draw out and unpack themes regarding one's lived teaching life. Personal positionings, over time, emerged as a crucial part of studying "one's self, one's actions, one's ideas, as well as the 'not self'" (Hamilton & Pinnegar, 1998, p. 238) as a means to explicate previously misunderstood privileges. The criticality of this self-study can be found in the ways that the relationships between power, authority, knowledge production, and contextual social relations are illuminated and mediated (Freire, 1996; Steinberg & Kincheloe, 2018; Kincheloe, 2008; Giroux 2011).

School as place situates many considerations of the self-study, whereby Alcoff (1991) suggests *place* may be a "*social* location, or a social identity" (p. 7)—the *place* of unfolding and enfolding of memories, encounters, and history within the confluence of past, present, and a possible future. Considering these moments reflexively through self-study has allowed for the critical illumination of some ways to afford future iterative interconnected possibilities in education. It is this ecological sensibility envisioned as a direct challenge to the reductionistic, fictitious simplification of classroom dynamics. A challenge to pedagogies that conjure a singular, prescriptive, and safe understanding of living classrooms—classrooms that are ever-emergent, continually adapting, and divergently redundant. These are spaces of the possible, of the not-yet-imagined; they can be the fertile locations of growth and change.

The shifts in leadership responsibilities as outlined by Bedard and Mombourquette (2015) served as implicit groundings for this self-study. Through the consideration of pedagogical metaphors (Gereluk et al., 2016) and associated entailments (Davis & Renert, 2013a, 2013b) within the evidence of the self-study, schema and paradigms, and the affordances allowed were considered. Ultimately, the self-study has emerged as *a story* of impact and possibility—perceptions of the subtle perturbative impacts on pedagogies and paradigms, and possibilities for the evolution of teaching pedagogies from reductionist and positivist towards enmeshed and relational and pedagogical possibilities of love. As Kahn and Kellner (2008) suggest, "education, at its best, provides the symbolic and cultural capital that empowers people to survive and prosper in an increasingly complex and changing world and the resources to produce a more cooperative, democratic, egalitarian, and just society" (p. 25). I believe we deserve this society.

This book sets out to share the story and journey towards self-knowledge for one school leader; however, the process will likely be applicable to others interested in social research. Through the recursive journey towards better understandings, I have come to a place of increased awareness of my relationality and better recognition of interconnected nature of all social interactions.

· 1 ·
SELF-STUDY AND AUTOBIOGRAPHY

Education is political. Education, regardless of the intention, inadvertently serves to promote the status and standing of groups in power and with privilege (Nganga & Kambutu, 2013). Education is the enactment[1] of societal understandings, beliefs, and values. When enacted in a good way, education may afford engaging, enlightening, and emancipatory possibilities—possibilities of hope and love. However, all education is necessarily an embodiment of past understandings. Put differently, while we may envision a possible future through education, enacted education is always enmeshed within our lived affective history and experience. The structures, curricula, and pedagogies of education come into being through the enmeshed experiences of the past and present. Educational leaders not only have the opportunity but the ethical and moral responsibility to evaluate, consider, and challenge how appropriate or adequate their inherited curricula (Tarc, 2011) are within the current and emerging cultural and collective context. Administrators are therefore called upon to make decisions through multiple lenses in a responsive manner that considers the past but creates the opportunity for their transformative work to become tacit and readily subsumable through future iterations of reinvention. Responsive, empathetic, compassionate, transformative administrators will likely possess the courage, resilience, and vision to support all learners by helping to disrupt hegemonic teaching paradigms through pedagogies of love.

Education embodying[2] and enacting historically adequate paradigms presupposes that effectiveness is preparing students for a known future by means of *ensuring* the learning of discrete and static pieces of knowledge—a knowing that is potentially understood by students as mutually exclusive and disconnected from other content area disciplines or classrooms. When language that supports absolutist and reductionistic metaphors for students is used, positivist binaries of learning are perpetuated to future generations—leaving no room for acceptable divergent alternative epistemologies. It is important to emphasize that the current hegemonic, positivistic, convergent, data-driven teaching paradigm is but one possibility for education, one of the multiplicity of possibilities for education.

As part of this reflexive engagement, I worked to unpack how I have come to *my* current educational moment. My historical (re)collection is informed by experiential echoes through critical personal history self-study, and was the (re)consideration of how I may afford disruptive learning opportunities. This self-study has served as a reflexive means to better understand how my experiences in education—both formal and informal—have impacted the ways in which I have come to understand education. I now better understand that part of my process of becoming[3] (Britzman, 2003) is an ongoing desire to better understand how and in which ways administrators can facilitate/offset/disrupt current understandings of education and the possibilities that these understandings may afford.

Through this research process I have become better prepared to support dialogical experiences that may occasion for a more connected, complexified, messy, collective, and emergent understanding of education—an education that incorporates wholeness.[4] As a principal I am aware that administrators' roles have changed greatly throughout past decades (see Bedard & Mombourquette, 2015), and that administrators' impacts on student learning are second only to those of classroom teachers (Adams, 2016). It is my hope that by sharing this bricolage of critical personal history self-study[5] I may be able to impact both administrators' and teachers' paradigms, opening metaphors for ancillary possibilities.

My Short Autobiography

My story is written in a standard left justified manner that represents the (re)collection of my autobiography. There are insertions of thinking about things as I went back and reflected on my affective self; these are right justified and italicized. Writing in an alternative manner to the standard script was a way for me to push back against the hegemony of acceptable representation that I experienced during my academic career. I took the opportunity to use my autobiography as the location for an alternative form of writing because it is the location where I share and reflect on some of my most personal thoughts and experiences and the format fit well with the recursive way that I engaged in reflexivity. In this spirit I position myself through my story, the best that I can remember it, through a memory/wisdom impacted by future events, through a lens of today. The *truthing* (Little Bear, 2000) comes as the result of what I believe, know, and share as part of my truth.

No one can ever know for certain what someone else knows. The only thing one can go on is what the other human being shares or says to others. And, in all of this, there is an underlying assumption that a person is reporting an event in the way he or she experienced it… there is a strong expectation that everyone will share his or her truth (actually, "truthing" is a better concept) because people depend on each other's honesty to create a holistic understanding. (Little Bear, 2000, p. 80)

I was born during the dying days of the Cold War, which was not a Canadian conflict, but certainly had great influence over the pedagogical and curricular focuses of the Western Eurocentric world.

The influences of the Sputnik era were everywhere.
Positivism.
The belief that we could engineer a better tomorrow.
The arrogance that humans knew better about creating a world than nature's evolution.
Math and science focuses were prevalent in schools.

I was born into a middle-class, white family with an older sister, married parents, and married grandparents. My father held a secure management position with the British Columbia's Provincial Parks Service.

He was an immigrant from Southern Rhodesia.
My grandparents had moved there via Cypress.
I still know very little about the family's history,
And now the ones who knew have passed.

He had no discernable accent—
So, we were the right kind of white.
But is it ever really that simple?
My mother stayed at home and ran a part-time daycare.
Her family was from Manitoba and Vancouver,
For generations, I think.
As children, we wanted for nothing. At the very least, we were unaware that we needed anything; we certainly did not go hungry.
It was not until I had moved away from home that I realized how tight money must have been.
There were several occasions where contract negotiations resulted in lengthy job action—
Challenging for a young, family.
My mom made do. She made our clothes.
She also ran a daycare.
We thought that they were "play" clothes, but it was probably all they could afford.
They were good parents.
They are good grandparents.
I was the only male born in my immediate family—the only one to carry on the family name—a hope for the future, perhaps. A hope of what, I am not sure?
No pressure though.
I can remember hearing similar statements at family gatherings.
Usually, they came with a hair rub from male family members on my dad's side of the family.
We lived in a small home in Hammond, a suburb of Maple Ridge, in a home of which I have absolutely no recollection.
I have been told that the day after Mt. St. Helens erupted,
Our neighbourhood resembled a winter scene—a blanket of ash covered everything.
I have no recollection.
As the result of my father's work, we moved from the lower mainland to the Central Okanagan immediately after my youngest sister was born.
I have heard that both my older sister and I wanted a brother,
We were quite disappointed when my parents brought her home.
We even tried to convince them to give her a boy's name, to no avail.
We spent the first month living in a camper on the back of our family truck because the house that we were to live in had not been completed on time.

It must have been quite a scene, a young mother with three kids and a large dog living in a camper at the boat launch parking lot of South Okanagan Provincial Park. My father's office was in the building up on the hillside above this particular park, so he was able to come down to visit during lunchtime.

Stories—I certainly cannot corroborate any of this.
My thoughts woven together through hearing the reflections and recollections of others' truths.

I am sure that this helped my mother maintain her sanity—at least for a bit. After the first month, this arrangement became onerous. With the occupation date for the house pushed back yet again, we packed up our moveable home for a new-to-us, temporary rental home on the other side of town. I have very few memories of this time of my life; however, I can remember the tree in the front of this new home clearly. It's gnarled trunk and enormous canopy swallowed the sunlight of hot summer afternoons and the nut pods the tree produced were too tempting for my older sister and I to resist playing with. We would hunt through the remnants of what the birds had not eaten off the ground in our front yard. Occasionally we found an intact, solid walnut inside one of these fleshy globes; however, most of the time all we found was more ammunition to fire back and forth at each other—ammunition that as the result of its chemical make-up turned our skin a silvery black color.

A color that it turned out, also got a "wait til your father gets home"—
reminders to "quit getting filthy" as the result of playing.

I was a young child, occasionally a "pain-in-the-ass," rambunctious even, but a child none-the-less—securely attached (Kobak & Madsen, 2008), and loved. Only four months late, the house was finally finished. We moved into our new home in an era of violently rising interest rates and foreclosures; the up and down of which, we were lucky enough to lock-in before and re-finance afterwards.

Many families lost their homes.
Are we moving into a similar era?

I shared a room upstairs with my youngest sister. I can remember singing songs to her occasionally when we were both in our beds for the night. We loved each other.

We were close then.
We have grown apart. Still family, but we have grown apart.
There are too many things to disagree about.
As we learn more and change, it can be hard to be around family. (hooks, 1994)

This was our family home. I remember it with mostly fond memories. Both my older sister and I walked to elementary school from this home.

She is a nurse.
A fierce advocate for our family.
An excellent mother.
And my brother-in-law is an excellent father.
Who am I to make that discernment?

It was only a few blocks away, at first my mother supervised, and later we went on our own. We spent our summers camping, either in campgrounds near our home, or out on the covered patio outside of our kitchen. That area of the Okanagan was a great place to watch a late-night thunderstorm followed by a massive downpour of rain. The fall was spent back in school, but the winter weekends were spent on the ski hills. I loved skiing. I have many vivid memories of skiing.

I think that we only went a few times,
But that is what I remember about those days.
I think that we loved it there.

In November of my third-grade year my father earned a promotion that moved us to the far northeast of the province, where the days were short and the cold was long.

I am certain that I didn't want to move—
Moving us from our friends—
Moving us from the only life that I knew.
And when my nostrils froze shut for the first time, I was certain of it.

It was a minus 40 degrees Celsius wake up call. There were time warnings for how long it would take to get frostbite; trucks ran all night so that they could work in the morning. My parents, I assume because they were hoping that this location would be quite temporary, decided to rent a home rather than buying. Luckily for them, and for us too, this bet paid off. By summer that year, a mere six months later, we were moving again.

We were far from being a military family,
But it is always hard to invest in friendships,
Then move away—especially as a child.

This time we moved to the town of Smithers in the north central part of the province.

Smithers was a beautiful place in the Bulkley River valley situated at the leeward side of Hudson Bay Mountain—a mountain with a ski hill none-the-less.

I connected to the area immediately.

Mountains, waterfalls, very few people.
For a self-proclaimed outgoing introvert, it was a perfect place to grow up.
Some of my happiest memories are connected to this location.

I attended Walnut Park Elementary School for three years. It was a relatively new clean school only a one-block walk from our home. We rarely saw our extended family. I am certain that it was because of the 1,200 km drive from the lower mainland where the majority of them lived.

This is different than Jennifer's family. They are all close.
I envy that.
Recently, I have reconnected with some.

Middle school years are awkward for everyone, and in Smithers the middle school was no exception. Chandler Park School was a grade 7 and 8 school. Set off on the opposite side of town from our home, the school might have well been on a different planet. Pre, post, and full-onset puberty raged rampantly in what I now say are probably two of the most challenging grades to teach. All we needed was a fence with barbed wire and some guard outposts to complete the institutionalization. The academic portion of school was easy; I can't remember ever feeling challenged. I was pretty small for my age—a small, white, middle-class male—socially awkward, lacking confidence, and chubby.

I wasn't awkward when it came to academics; in fact, this was where I felt confident—
Which is what likely got me into trouble.
I remember feeling awkward.
Middle school was tough for me.
Girls didn't notice me.

I can remember getting "tuned-in" several times in the field on my way home, until one of the cooler kids in my grade stepped up and called the other kid out, putting an end to my ordeal.

I was thankful.
How did nobody else see?
Years later, I remember seeing the kid that used to pick on me relentlessly.
I thought he would be bigger.

I still loved being outdoors—the wilderness, camping, hiking, and skiing—I felt a connection to the outdoors, to nature, and to the wilderness.

I showed up to high school in September looking to start anew: new clothes, new haircut, and apparently sporting a few extra inches in height that I had gained over the summer.

Few of my peers recognized me.
It was pretty great feeling like the new kid in the school.
I worked hard in gym class and was asked by one of the teachers to try-out for the wrestling team. This was a major turning point in my life—a substantial identity shift.
I was good at something other than academics.
It is amazing how outward appearances are so very important to all of us.
Even if we try not to admit it.
I lived for wrestling.
Girls even started noticing me.
Many of my winter weekends were spent traveling throughout Western Canada or the United States for wrestling, or up the ski hill.
I did well in the sciences and social studies with little effort—anything that was logic-based—I learned through making coherence of the world and the word (Freire, 1996). But I had to work hard to do well in language arts. The writing I produced was formulaic, less than inspired, and rarely memorable. I could hear what I wanted to say but could never articulate it in a manner that made sense.
This part of my identity has followed me all of the way through university,
And even through my first round of graduate school.
I existed with questioned consciousness to writing,
I enjoyed writing, but disliked being evaluated on structures that didn't make sense.
I had to work my identity to fit within the academic context—
A multiplicity of seemingly incoherent world-curricula (Lessard, Caine, & Clandinin, 2015):
Success in the sciences and sports, and failure in writing.
I met my *life* partner in the summer after grade 11. She has been my inspiration for almost two-thirds of our lives. Our identies enmeshed within each other's.
It hasn't been easy.
We are figuring life out together—negotiating,
27 years, 22 of which married,
And let me tell you, the one thing that I know,
marriage is Fucking Hard.
We have been through so much together. Good and bad.
But it is worth it.
Every day I am grateful. I am lucky.
Two beautiful kids—they inspire us to be better.
Here we are, still together.

She inspires me—to be better. She is why I can write.
She is my trusted one (King, 2010) who critiques my work and tells me if it makes sense.
Unknowingly, a friend of mine thought that there was a cute girl in the 10th grade that he would like to meet. I didn't know her personally but felt that I could make the introduction.
The introduction happened, but apparently it was of her to me.
I hear that he is doing well too.
Smithers, located in the Bulkley Valley, on the unceded traditional territory of the Gitxsan and Wet'suwet'en Peoples near the reserve of Moricetown.
The Carrier people.
Originally named Witset; renamed for a missionary.
Hegemonic narcissism.
Famous for its gaff fishing,
Now nets replace traditional ways, to be more protective of the fish.
White fishermen delightedly pay 10 dollars for their own spot on "Idiot Rock"
A tiny, densely populated, outcropping where huge fish can be hooked—
Wrapping around everyone else's lines—rarely is a fish landed.
Aptly named location from my outsider (Innes, 2009) ethnographic interpretation.
This area lies in the middle of British Columbia's Highway 16, which has been identified as the *Highway of Tears* (see McDiarmid, 2019). This name has come as the result of the large number of Missing and Murdered Indigenous Women and Girls on this section of highway.
I never knew these women were going missing—being murdered.
Perhaps we—the white people—didn't want to know.
Perhaps the media's white racist perspective helped formulated our white racist perspectives.
Likely these perspectives were already there.
It was a white, female, tree planter—
Abducted while hitch-hiking—that brought attention to this horrific and ongoing epidemic,
Not one of the many Indigenous women or girls.
We lost several kids from my school during the four years that I attended high school. Some of these losses came as the result of unfortunate accidents; some came as direct or indirect result of drug and alcohol use—all of them were celebrated with ceremonies.
For the white kids it was always an unfortunate tragedy—a chance to learn.
For the Indigenous kids...well,

No one seemed surprised.
We were all racist—we still are?
Will my children be?

There was a girl, a year older than me. We both worked part-time at the same restaurant. She was always very nice to me; she always said hello at school as well. One day she missed her shift at work. She was not at school the next week. The adults I knew did not seem to be all that concerned. Months later her body was discovered a few kilometers out of town. The investigation continued, but nothing was found. No one was charged. Still nothing.

Are we all innocent if we don't remember?
I still think about her occasionally.
Who would she have been?

I was lucky, privileged in a way that was apparent for others to see. Throughout high school, I saw many of the wild parts of Northern British Columbia and its provincial parks: Tatlatui by float plane; Spatsizi by helicopter, hiking, jet boat, and float plane; Mount Edziza by helicopter; Kluane by DC-3 and float plane; Tweedsmuir by jet boat and float plane, and The Queen Charlotte Islands (Now more accurately known as Haida Gwaii with Gwaii Haanas Provincial Park), just to name a few.

This is where I learned to love nature, prior to wanting to save it.
(Gruenewald, 2003)
This love is what I want for my children.
This is also where I first recognized the complete destruction of ecosystems,
Strip mining,
Clear-cutting.
So much devastation—
Out of sight—
So obvious from the air.
No one seemed to mind.
Do they now?

Before my grade 12 year, we spent two weeks canoeing the Spatsizi and Stikine Rivers in Northern B.C. In the middle of nowhere, we saw nobody else for two full weeks. What an amazing experience. Few people ever get to see this area of the country.

If you haven't had the experience, it is hard to understand.
I felt a connection to place there like no other.
Every breathe, every sound, every sight,

A connection that I haven't found in any urban environment. A love of interconnection.

The summer before university, I worked with a contractor surveying the Bulkley Forest Timber Supply. Up at 4 a.m. every day, in a helicopter, dropped in the middle of nowhere, surveying, then hiking back out.

If I could choose any job, this is the one I would choose to do now.
The mountain pine beetle has since devastated this timber supply,
So many factors:
Climate change,
Forest mismanagement.
The reductionist belief that humans could apply a simple,
Positivist management approach to a complex ecosystem.
Were we doomed to fail?
We are finally beginning to listen to Indigenous Knowledge Keepers and Elders.
Is the acceptance and valuing of Indigenous knowledges coming too late?

At the end of that summer my heart broke for the first time, when I left to go to university, leaving the only home that I have ever known. I spent my first year of post-secondary at Simon Fraser University. Funny thing about wrestling scholarships, they expect a great deal from student athletes. My first year away from home I wrestled in a National Association Intercollegiate Athletics 142 lb. weight-class, when I had wrestled at 150 lb. in high school.

I have fought with this part of my identity for years,
Weight and image,
I weighed 170 lb. wrestled 142 lb.—
Winning and losing depending on the year.

I had academic studies; but most of all, I had freedom. Pre-Skype, pre-cell phone, pre-high-speed Internet, I was a white, heterosexual, privileged, middle-class, university educated male.

I would call home from the payphone at the end of the hall in residence.
I could afford it—my parents funded my calls and subsidized tuition.
I paid for the remainder of my schooling.

This lasted for one year, then I took a year off to work and figure out the future. A year later *we* moved to Vancouver, cohabitating for the first time in our lives. Now I had to consider someone else other than just myself. We moved. Jennifer and Me.

My parents were part of the United Church
So it wasn't 'in sin'
Depending who in our families you asked.

We attended more school together, first Douglas College in Coquitlam, then Camosun College in Victoria, and finally the University of Victoria where we both graduated with our first degrees. Somewhere in there, we were married—in a United Church.

To this day I don't know why.
Even then religion was not part of my life—
Spirituality yes, but certainly not religion.
In fact, a-theism was a more likely belief.
Perhaps, it was to meet family expectations?

We purchased a home. I was a white, married, heterosexual, able bodied, home-owning, student, and soon-to-be educator, living paycheque-to-paycheque. Until I was injured in a workplace accident and learned what it meant to be temporarily non-able bodied. I spent the good part of five months laying on the floor in the living room, rehabilitating.

Back injuries make you reconsider many of your life choices.
Apparently wrestling, tree planting, and installing hardwood floors are not good for your back.
I feel it more as I get older.

We lived apart for much of our first and fifth years of marriage, which made for all sorts of emotional and relational struggles.

Yet here we are, feisty and still figuring it out,
In love.
Continually (re)defining what that means.

In our sixth year of marriage, we moved to Calgary. I followed Jennifer and her teaching career. It was here I also earned my bachelor's degree in education, which along with my other degrees from The University of Victoria allowed me to be immediately hired into a high school.

Apparently being white, male, educated, and able to coach sports made me employable.
I have never once attended my own post-secondary graduation.
4 of them.
There was always something more important.
Work, family…
Each distinction attained through hard work—
Did I earn this or was it white privilege?
Binaries?… Or?… Both and yes….
How much did hard work contribute to my success?
Is it possibly that simple?

I connected immediately with the principal of the school in High River. It was a great school. He was a great administrator. But I struggled with many of the prescriptive and perscriptive pedagogies that my colleagues felt were the only way to educate students in mathematics and the sciences.

I worked long hours during the first years:
Coaching
Preparing
I think that I did well.
I held tightly to the belief that "what teachers say and do every day can have a tremendous impact on the lives of their students" (Nieto, 2006, p. 3).
Because "language is not a neutral transmitter of a universal reality" (Sensoy & DiAngelo, 2012, p. 48).
So much power—hopefully less hegemonic as the years pass.
Hopefully for the good.
I have feared every day that the silent voices of students that struggled were negatively impacted by my pedagogy and practice.
I care. I work hard to build relationships, in the best ways that I know how. But it took years of learning, experience, and wisdom to understand that there are alternative pedagogies.

Two years later in 2009, our first son was born.

He is so beautiful, outgoing, and talented—
He inspires me to be better every day.
I wish that all parents felt that way.
Unfortunately, as the result of my teaching and administrative career, I know that there are many who don't.
So many children—
Neglected,
Ignored,
Abused.
Born innocent.
How can we support all students?
We need to love them all and embody this love through our pedagogies.
All children are our collective responsibility, the responsibility of the community.
"How are we recognizing the severity of issues for certain bodies despite the fact that the issues which we are all concerned affect all students?" (Dei, 2008, p. 359)

We bought an older house in High River and renovated it.

Jennifer joked that she courted High River throughout her first pregnancy.
A small town, with a small-town feel.

Amazing people. Great friends.
It reminded us both of our childhood homes.
We were living in the basement while we worked on the upstairs. On the first night after we finished the renovation, sleeping upstairs for the first time, it must have been the right time, it was time to have our second child. We lived two blocks from the hospital, so we walked there. Our youngest son was born that day in 2011.
Outgoing, kind, sweet,
A daredevil, a bit of a troublemaker.
My mother tells me that I earned this one.
We could be twins.
Now a father for the second time—I was a white male, still living paycheque-to-paycheque, heterosexual, married, able bodied, and an employed educator under a tenured continuous contract. We completed our master's degrees in 2013, as part of the same cohort. Part of the time, we had our youngest son in tow, with a lot of support from my father-in-law and his wife—known to the boys as, Grandpa and Nona.
They are amazing with the boys.
I don't think that we would have completed our masters' degrees without them.
Not sure that we could manage life without them.
We had a lot of support from cohort members.
They let us do projects together, knowing that we had our hands full.
Prior to the completion, frustrated with administration changes we took work overseas.
Apparently, this is the leading cause of teachers leaving their workplace.
As a relatively new administrator, I take this to heart.
But change is hard.
I finished my final paper on the night of June 19, 2013; writing and submitting from my classroom around 10 p.m. We had already rented our home because we were moving in August.
I have never seen rain like that in Alberta before.
It was on the next day that the town of High River was evacuated due to flood.
The tenants' property was saved.
Everything that we had owned
After 18 years together—13 years married, 4 with children—
Was stored in the basement.
Now filled with five feet of sewage back-flow—
Everything was destroyed.

We were lucky—our house was saved. Others were not so lucky. We repaired the damage; we have moved on. We try to move on.

We deal with the damage,
I can't sleep when it rains.
We repaired the basement.
Air tests,
Restoration.
We just sold the house last year,
Putting behind us our past—another family's future.
It added stress on our relationship, often pushing us to the edge, but here we still are—
figuring it out, in love—as a family.

After all of this, we are happy. We have wonderful friends. We have been afforded great opportunities. We are busy with all of the activities of two middle school aged boys.

Loved by so many.
Not sure how they identify: heterosexual, homosexual, bisexual, two-spirit…it doesn't really matter
Loved without reservation.
I will do my best to make sure they our children know they are loved.
Everyday.

We are now learning more about identity: Jennifer working to better understand her Métis family heritage, me trying to understand how I can help support her and our children in this learning journey.

Histories and cultures lost due to intentional hiding from horrific government policies.
Families torn apart,
Cultures lost,
Identities changing and evolving.
They are both Métis males, middle-classed, privileged and learning to be humble.
So loved.

We travel, we spend the summers camping together. The boys love to be outside, on the beach, in the woods, covered in dirt, as they should be. We love to be there with them—they inspire us.

Many summers involved writing.
Each of us sacrificing to complete graduate degrees: Jennifer, PhD. (finished in 2020),
me an EdD. (finished in 2021).

Supporting each other. Hopefully not resenting each other.
COVID was hard. Is hard. For everyone. Its impacts will be felt for years to come. Emotional. Financial. Relational, and marital. I don't really know what else to say. Everyone lived a different experience through the last two years.

I can't help but feel broken.
I am tired.
Stress.
Anxiety.
Fear.
Change.
We were lucky. Financially stable. Supported.
I could have done better.
I should have known better.
I probably should have done better.
How do we know?

Jennifer has now completed her doctorate. Focusing on youth and their experiences during and after the High River Flood. Her work incorporates Indigenous pedagogies and leans towards her future work with Service First research focuses. A new position as an Assistant Professor with a nomination for a Canada Research Chair.

This work will take her to reserve communities and northern Alberta communities.
This work will make a difference.
It is inspiring work. She is inspiring.
Her work and her story have impacted everything about me and the ways that I have come to know and understand teaching.

I completed an EdD. focusing on how pedagogies of love can provide inclusive and divergent possibilities for all learners. My employer now title me as a Principal of a K-9 school.

Title Me: Imposter? Time will Tell.
Worries, but motivates,
Make change through perturbations,
Small pushes to well established culture.

We have sold our home in High River and moved to Calgary—Mohkínstsis as known by the Blackfoot People and as it probably should be—part of treaty 7 territory and the home to Métis Nation, Region 3.

Shorter commutes.
Memories of loss no longer exist in concrete and wood structures.
But they do remain in our hearts and souls.

They do remain.
I am white, very privileged, middle-classed, still paycheque-to-paycheque, incredibly lucky, a father, university educated, an educator, an administrator, a leader, a coach. Married—constantly redefining that definition.
It is amazing how we have grown together,
Changed together,
For so many years. Together more years than we haven't been.
Self-study and autobiography required me to reflect, reconsider, and (re)remember.
Regrets. Mistakes.
But happy. As we understand ourselves better, we can't help but question life trajectories.
But we support each other. In all that we do.
I am a partner, working on being a better partner, currently able bodied, healthy and of sound mind, happy, and loved.
But, is it ever that simple?

Context and My First Positioning

We teach, with no knowledge or certainty about what consequences our actions as teachers will have. At the heart of teaching about and across cultural differences is the impossibility of designating precisely what actions, selves, or knowledges are "correct" or "needed." (Ellsworth, 1997, p. 17)

The context of this research is not simply a location or understanding. The location for this research is Southern Alberta; however, the context is entangled within my own affective life experiences in Western Canada and the experiences of those that impacted me in subtle and not-so-subtle ways. Through multiple positionings[6] within the first sections of this book, I share myself with readers so that they may better understand who I am and why I feel the necessity to initiate this study. Later on, as part of my critical personal history self-study project I used positionings and other personal artifacts of my autobiographical narrative writing as research evidence.

I position myself in this work so that I may be better understood. I position myself to share why I chose to write what it is that I write, why I attend to what it is that I attend to; and where my biases lay. As Wilson (2008) states, one's *relational accountability* cannot be disconnected from their writing, and "requires that you know a lot more about me before you can begin to understand my work" (p. 12). I write from Treaty 7 territory in Southern Alberta, from the traditional territory of the Blackfoot Confederacy (comprising the Siksika, Piikani, and Kainai First Nations), the Tsuut'ina First Nation, and the Îyârhe Nakoda (including the Chiniki, Bearspaw, and Wesley First Nations) and the Métis Nation of Alberta Region 3—a recognition that I would not have made during my youth. I am privileged, white, currently able bodied—another recognition that I would not have made until recently. Having grown up in northern British Columbia, I have a strong connection to the land. I am a teacher-turned-administrator who struggles with the ways that enacted absolutist, disconnected, and reductionist curricula are still pervasive within Western Canadian and more specifically Albertan[7] education—the sacrosanct ways that things are done, lost in time.

I continue to struggle with the ways that teachers and their reputations may be disconnected from that of effective pedagogy which exist in a state of stasis through public persona—whether good or bad. Britzman (2003) describes these persistent social perceptions of the effective teacher when she writes that these "stereotypes engender a static and hence repressed notion of identity as something already out there, a stability that can be assumed" (p. 29). Collectively, pedagogies that are unchallengeable for fear of "teacher bashing," removing autonomy, or questioning professional codes of conduct, become cultural within schools because of their potentially ancient relevance. I have witnessed some progressive reflexive impacts that teacher-as-action-researcher has had on individual classrooms; however, I have noticed that this new lens has empowered many others to justify their positivistic pedagogies to be the most effective—perpetuating *best practices* discourses (Friesen, 2019).

I have set aside my voice as a teacher over the past seven years since moving into the role of administrator. This has caused a dramatic shift in my identity. While it would be egocentric of me to claim that I was an effective mathematics and physics teacher, I was not the kind that focused on surface-level understandings. I consider myself to be a pragmatist who broke down the theory/practice dichotomy, and I had no problem challenging colleagues that I felt had more teacher-centered pedagogies. I worked hard to embody a pedagogy of *walking beside* students on a collective journey of reflection to disruptively transform understandings. Now, not having *teacher* as part of my identity (both inside school and out) has removed my expertise. As Daughenbaugh and Shaw (2013) suggest, "identity creation is a process based on past acts which produces an illusion for society as a result of both understated and obvious pressures" (p. 18); as a result, I have become incredibly aware that it is not me, but rather the community that defines my identity within education.

My new role has afforded me the opportunity to observe many teachers who build relationships focused on hope and care. Through dialogue with these masters of their craft, we are able to perturbate a co-evolution[8] of our praxis, as Ellsworth (1997) states, "communicative dialogue drives forward mutual understandings as a pedagogical ideal" (p. 15). These teachers understand all too well the precarious hierarchy that can exist in classrooms comprised of students and teachers, for "we are not equals in the classroom. Teachers have more power than students. And…it is easy for teachers to misuse that power" (hooks, 2010, p. 114). There are, however, many others whose classrooms are clearly identified as the teacher's space, where students must attend and comply, putting the role of these teachers at the top of a hierarchy with students as subjects passively consuming already clearly stated knowledge. Doll (1993) criticizes this pedagogy where "from the first grade on, curriculum is considered in terms of units arranged in linear order. Learning, itself, is defined in terms of the number of units covered, mastered, *accumulated* [emphasis added]. Such a view does not facilitate considering curriculum as a transformative process" (p. 38).

Teaching with the illusion of certainty that a linear, cause-effect, top-down paradigm affords a sense of safety that the potential messiness of a more divergent paradigm cannot (Biesta, 2013). Absolutism and positivism enacted in education have falsely reduced learning and teaching to interactions of simplicity (Weaver, 1948), which allows educators to feel that they can be the direct cause of the student learning. As a result, students and their behaviors can be reduced to simplistic, controlled variables with no agency. When education is understood in this manner, the curriculum may be prescriptively interpreted through a singular disembodied, historied lens of the teacher with the intention of transmission to a fictitiously normative audience, and, by its effective implementation good teaching is defined. Through this mechanistic metaphor of education, the control (management) of a classroom and the implementation (teaching) and attainment (learning) of a predefined static knowledge set (curriculum) are directly correlated to a teacher's effectiveness (Hargreaves & Ainscow, 2015). Therefore, learning, teaching, and a perception of safety are directly related to control—oppressive control over what is being taught, what is being learned, and how it is being measured. This may be the reason why "educators turn to slogans or commonsense solutions in their search for (impossible) ways out" (Ellsworth, 1997, p. 11) of corners they are stuck in by axioms of education. In a prescribed model of education, all aspects of education: teaching, learning, students, classrooms, etc. are foundationally connected to the false belief in a simplistic, reductionistic, decontextualized, and rationalistic existence that can be objectively measured.

There is a current prevalence and popularization of assurance models of education in the context of Albertan public schools. These models seem to attempt to verify for educational stakeholders the worth and effectiveness of public education and its educators. The veiled attempts to quantify educational successes, in the short term, through standardized commensurable measures ignore the plethora of incommensurable supports educators afford for students every day.

How can we disrupt the deeply entrenched belief in Albertan public schools that education is something imposed, top-down, to and on students? How can new frameworks overcome the *banking model* of education (Freire, 1996), whereby when students have acquired an acceptable amount of educational currency, they are deemed ready for the *real world*? How can we decenter taken-for-granted, common-sensical visions of education that require negative-feedback-focused, linear trajectories to achieve static knowledge of that which is already known? How can cultures of teaching shift to incorporate transformative processes through considerations of student coherence-making opportunities, reflexively negotiated, affording for ever-evolving conceptual understandings of the yet-to-be known? Davies (2006) posits, "we must take responsibility for examining the documents and discursive practices that are taken for granted in our schools and universities and ask what conditions of possibilities are they creating and maintaining for us and for our students" (p. 436). We must challenge, discuss, and unlearn much of the language and beliefs of our difficult curricular inheritance (Tarc, 2011).

Research Focus

In this research I explored how my understandings of personal educational experiences have impacted and transformed my pedagogical understandings, ultimately bringing me to a better awareness of the current moment. By critically questioning perceived experiences reflexively through a recalled history and with critical friends, paying particular attention to metaphors for education, teaching, and learning, I better understand myself and my perceptions of education. Metaphors and possible associated entailments served as inroads to paradigms and how and to what extent these paradigms' implicit affordances may promote and perpetuate the enactments of reductionist and positivist educational pedagogies. Having a better understanding of possibilities afforded through education allows me to openly disrupt these paradigms and pedagogies through dialogue which may support in divergent, constructive, and transformative learning opportunities within the context of school communities. I hope that as educators begin to imagine the possibilities of divergent curriculum, they will begin to become comfortable with the uncomfortable—the complex, divergent, messy, and self-sustaining nature of a curriculum that is empowering to all learners towards the not-yet-imagined.

Research Topic

Contemporary metaphors about teaching and schooling support and perpetuate absolutist and positivist language of teacher impact in terms of a cause-and-effect relationship in terms of *best* practice discourses (Gereluk et al., 2016; Hattie, 2011; Marzano, Frontier, & Livingston, 2011; Marzano, 2007; Friesen, 2019). These discourses propagate negative feedback and assurance-focused understandings of pedagogies that close possibilities for alternative understandings or opportunities. To maintain their scientific relevance impacts must be measurable. "Something is not measurable it is not scientific" (Little Bear, 2000, p. 81). According to Friesen (2019) "best practices discourse provides no opportunity for improvement or reimagining otherwise. It also leaves no space for considering the learning needs of the learner or the subject discipline; therefore, within education it seems to operate as a pedagogical foreclosure." While there is research and literature that supports the possibilities of paradigm shifts away from convergent absolutism towards that of divergent ecological sensibilities (Doll, 1993; Quinn, 2018a)—a complex relationship between all agents with the potential of transforming pedagogy (Davis et al., 2008, 2015)—little of this seems to gain traction within current classroom pedagogies and teacher paradigms focused on systemic accountability and assurances through data.

Research Problem

The metaphors that teachers hold for current understandings of their role define their relationships to knowledge and learners (Sfard, 1994; Weber &

Mitchell, 1995: Austin, 1996; Davis et al., 2008, 2015). If these teaching metaphors perpetuate a static understanding of teaching and learning they are likely to limit teachers' abilities to be reflexive (Lyle, 2017). Within classrooms and schools, language and dialogues that perpetuate simplistic dualisms and dichotomies are rarely challenged through disruptive pedagogies that serve to ameliorate accepted practices (Davis & Sumara, 2007; Ellsworth, 1997). In fact, Britzman (2003) suggests that rarely does a teacher's pedagogy look different from that which they have experienced because "it is taken for granted that we all know what a teacher is and does" (p. 27).

Positivistic uses of statistics and effect size calculations with the hope of effectively optimizing teaching practice for the betterment of society are problematic because this reductionistic application of data ignores the complexity of classrooms, context, and collective interactions. According to Biesta (2013), reducing human behaviors to positivistic statistics "denies the fact that human beings have their own ways of being and thinking, their own reasons and motivations" (p. 3). When applied to any one student or classroom, statistics are likely to lose relevance because they are then taken out of context (Wilson, 2008). Could it be that the oppressiveness of commonsense understandings of what teaching is (Kumashiro, 2002; Giroux, 1997, 2011) continues to preserve static metaphors of teaching? Perhaps it is the absence of apparent viable alternatives to their current paradigms, many of which are renamed variants of past paradigms that support the continued popularity of absolutism and positivism. As such, this research has endeavored to afford for teacher and administrator informed, passionate, growth-minded (Dweck, 2007) paradigm shifts through reflexive awakenings—shifts from those that tend towards the static and dualistic to those ancillary possibilities that are ever-evolving.

Purpose

The purpose of this research was to illuminate alternative possibilities for education in Alberta that may serve to disrupt current rationalist, reductionist pedagogies and paradigms that are perpetuated by top-down expectations and associated popular literatures. The *Alberta Leadership Quality Standard* (Alberta Education, 2017a) and the Foundational Principles of High School Redesign (Alberta Education, 2018a) serve as current representations and enabling constraints of educational understandings within the province of Alberta, and while these representations are an evolution from previous iterations of bureaucratic documents, they still perpetuate many of the same paradigms. Through the process of this personal history self-study research, alternative possibilities for education are focused on by considering a multiplicity of epistemologies and world curricula (Lessard et al., 2015; Aoki, 2004); additionally, and the complex collectivity that is a reality of classrooms (Doll, 1993; Davis et al., 2008; Quinn, 2018b; Jones, 2013) has been illuminated with the hope that I may afford for curricula that are rooted in divergent ecological understandings.

Through transformed possibilities for education, teaching and learning would not be "about convergence onto a pre-established truth, but about divergence—about broadening what can be known and done" (Davis & Sumara, 2007, p. 64). Doll (1993) suggests that such a shift would make it so that "the focus would now be on a community dedicated to helping each individual, through critique and dialogue, to develop intellectual and social powers" (p. 174). Shifting paradigms would not negate the learning of content; rather, it will require an increased level of richness, recursion, relation, and rigor (Doll, 1993) by considering learning as reflexive processes. By supporting teachers in gaining comfort around the messiness that is the complexity of the classroom, they may begin to see their role as educators transforming to one that is ancillary and not causative (Doll, 1993). Educators who consider this critical and ecological framework may possibly create a space for pedagogies of hope and love (Freire, 1996, 1994; hooks, 1994, 2001, 2003, 2010).

Theoretical Framework

My theoretical framework exists in the confluence of the complex and critical. And, while I do not want to quantify how much each of these conceptual pieces influenced my paradigm, what I can say is that I understand the world to be irreducibly interconnected but look to challenge how educators and education interpret or ignore those connections through criticality.

As I was interested in better understanding my own perceptions and affective embodiments of education in a wholistic sense while looking towards the possibilities of a not-yet-known future, the intimately (inter/intra)-connected nature of complex adaptive systems and ecological sensibilities served as a conceptual framework for this research. The infinitely-evolutionary, dynamically-perturbative, tensioned lens of complex adaptive systems (Davis et al., 2008, 2012, 2015; Doll, 1993; Jones, 2013) of education, relationships, and schools as was used to better understand the enmeshed nature of my own affective recollections of education. The living dynamic relationships of ecological sensibilities (Sumara et al., 2001; Weber, 2017; Cajete, 1994) served to make coherence of messy educational experiences that had previously been considered to be safe and controlled—pedagogies transformed from those confidently known through goals of convergence towards divergence of possibilities.

As a major portion of this self-study was to (re)consider the hegemonic structures and politics that exist in education, critical pedagogy served as a conceptual framework for this research. The power-interrogating lens of criticality (Tristan, 2013; Giroux, 2011; Steinberg & Kincheloe, 2018; Freire, 1996; Carspecken, 2013) was the primary and overarching part of my framework.

Defining Critical, Criticalist, and Critical Pedagogy

While I could have defined *critical* in my glossary, I feel that it is important to provide an extended definition at this point in the book. Criticality, as I have come to understand it, is so deeply embedded within my thoughts, understandings, and paradigm that I often struggle to engage in any other manner. Initially I felt that engaging as a criticalist required a negative outlook; however, I have begun to understand that through love a critical lens can become a productive, growth-focused engagement. The next few paragraphs will help to clarify what it is that I understand acting, researching, and being critical can mean.

Through my experiences over the past few years, I have been able to formalize my current understandings of the criticality of my own pedagogy. I align my understandings of critical pedagogy with Paulo Freire (1996) when he shares that "to surmount the situation of oppression, people must first critically recognize its causes, so that through transforming action they can create a new situation, one which makes possible the pursuit of fuller humanity" (p. 29). I now better understand that all education and associated pedagogies are political, and as a result, the enactment of paradigms and what we believe about students will in turn define what possibilities may be afforded through education. By using the term *critical* and incorporating critical pedagogy, I adhere to the understandings of Freire (1996), Steinberg and Kincheloe

(2018), Giroux (2011), and the descriptions that Henry Giroux shares as part of an interview with Tristán (2013). It is worth quoting Henry Giroux at length to help clarify my current understandings of critical pedagogy.

> Critical pedagogy illuminates the relationships among knowledge, authority, and power. It draws attention to questions concerning who has control over the conditions for the production of knowledge, values, and skills, and it illuminates how knowledge, identities, and authority are constructed within particular sets of social relations. Similarly, it draws attention to the fact that pedagogy is a deliberate attempt on the part of educators to influence how and what knowledge and subjectivities are produced within particular sets of social relations. (para. 2)

In a concluding statement Giroux shares that critical pedagogy "is the outcome of particular struggles and is always related to the specificity of particular contexts, students, communities, available resources, the histories that students bring with them to the classroom, and the diverse experiences and identities they inhabit" (para. 2).

It is also worth referencing Kincheloe and McLaren (1994) at length when discussing ideas associated with being critical, and orienting my own criticality.

> We are defining a criticalist as a researcher or theorist who attempts to use her or his work as a form of social or cultural criticism and who accepts certain basic assumptions: that all thought is fundamentally mediated by power relations which are socially and historically constituted; that facts can never be isolated from the domain of values or removed from some form of ideological inscription; that the relationship between concept and object and signifier and signified is never stable or fixed and is often mediated by the social relations of capitalist production and consumption; that language is central to the formation of subjectivity (conscious and unconscious awareness); that certain groups in any society are privileged over others; and, although the reasons for this privileging may vary widely, the oppression which characterizes contemporary societies is most forcefully reproduced when subordinates accept their social status as natural, necessary or inevitable; that oppression has many faces and that focusing on only one at the expense of others (e.g. class oppression versus racism) often elides the interconnections among them; and finally that mainstream research practices are generally, although most often unwittingly, implicated in the reproduction of systems of class, race and gender oppression. (pp. 139-140)

Enacting critical pedagogy thus promotes critical reflexivity whereby teachers and students are challenged to engage in an "investigation of their social location in the world as well as their relationship with the world" (McLaren, 2015, p. 46). Classrooms and schools that allow for the enactment of critical pedagogies provide the "space for learners to act as agents of social change" (Colonna & Nix-Stevenson, 2013, p. 8).

Research Question

The primary research question defines the intention of this research study (the full list of research questions can be found in Chapter Three).

How can I use self-study to better understand Albertan education in this current moment, and how, and in what ways can my current pedagogical understandings allow for divergent future educational possibilities?

Methodology

Within this section, I outline my considerations regarding the methodologies for this self-study, which include discussions around both ethics and methodology. Weaving these two important considerations of the study together was both intentional and, I believe, inevitable. There are many ways that we can study our(selves) including: narrative, biography, autobiography, ethnography, autoethnography, and self-study, just to name a few. I have been drawn to self-study research because of its recursive, reflexive, and dialogical nature. Self-study research is challenging to define; however, self-study is rooted in the confluence of the self and the social. Samaras and Freese (2006) propose the principal characteristics of self-study as: situated inquiry; process; knowledge; multiple in theoretical stance, method, and purpose; and paradoxical (pp. 40-53). Samaras (2011) suggests that methodologically, self-study research can be considered to be composed of a five foci framework (see Table 4): personal situated inquiry; critical collaborative inquiry; improved learning; a transparent and systemic research process; and, knowledge generation and presentation (pp. 72-73). LaBoskey (2004) suggests that the self-study is mainly qualitative and may include, but not limited to, narrative, dialogical, and arts-based methods.

As I share throughout the following section, and expand on further in Chapter Three, I believe there is no best or most appropriate methodology that can be undertaken when considering qualitative social research—only an evolving understanding of how methodologies may support the relationality and ethical responsibility of the researcher. I understand qualitative research as an inherently intimate, experiential, contextual, and transformative engagement—methodologies as entangled and in tension with ethics and relationality. In this context, the research study was undertaken through a bricolage of qualitative methodologies (Steinberg, 2012a).

Throughout the considerations for this study, the research approaches that fit ethically and relationally are critical. Carspecken (2013) posits that "'critical' qualitative research is one of several genres of inquiry into non-quantifiable features of social life" (p. 3). Steinberg (2012b) suggests that all qualitative research by nature is critical. She continues by suggesting that "we believe that research is a social theoretical act, and that it must be headlined by a socially just and equitable praxis. We believe that research must be contextual and is tentative in its surroundings" (p. ix). It is precisely this recognition of context, location, and place that I looked to foreground my discussion around methodological intentions and aspirations.

I believe human realities to be socially, psychologically, spiritually, and relationally constructed. Through reflexive considerations of self-study, I have come to better understand that my past experiences may serve as constraints to how I enact present moments. I envision the future's possibilities as mediated through a tacit confluence of considerations of affective experiences: contextual adequacy, relational similarity, and hopeful disruption. I feel that objective realities cannot exist unless the complexity and multiplicities of social interactions, intentions, and motivations are ignored. I feel that all interactions and experiences serve to disrupt and expand what it is that we understand as true or possible. As a result, I understand all social realities to be one of an infinite number of possible perceived social realities, each similar but varied enough to serve as initial conditions that may cause significantly different trajectories throughout time, space, and place.

I see myself and my theoretical positioning as a tension between social constructivism and complexivism—an ongoing struggle between a safe, convergent hegemonic absolutism and an unsettling, messy, experienced relativism. I discuss my epistemology and ontology further in Chapter Three. I position myself within this study through extensive experiential knowledges in the context as a K-12 teacher and administrator in Alberta and through this research project have worked to legitimize my personal voice publicly through critical reflection. As Loughran and Northfield (1998) posit:

> Reflection is a personal process of thinking, refining, reframing, and developing actions. Self-study takes these processes and makes them public, thus leading to another series of processes that need to reside outside the individual. Self-study can be considered as an extension of reflection on practice, with aspirations that go

> beyond reflection and even professional development and move to wider communication and consideration of ideas, i.e., the generation and communication of new knowledge and understanding. Reflection is important in self-study but it alone is not self-study. Self-study involves reflection on practice. (p. 15)

Using recalled dialogical experiences, recollections, written narratives, autobiography, and witnessings as data within this self-study necessitated a bricolage of methodologies (Kincheloe, 2001, 2005b; Steinberg, 2012a) including: self-study (LaBoskey, 2004; Samaras, 2011; Samaras et al., 2004; Samaras & Freese, 2006; Bullough & Pinnegar, 2001, 2004; Clandinin & Connelly, 2004; Whitehead, 2004), narrative and stories (Goodson & Gill, 2011; Kitchen, 2005; Cruikshank, 2000), and autobiography (Grumet, 1990; Clandinin & Connelly, 1990, 2004).

Self-study by nature is a critical research methodology because it may afford for a possible reconceptualization of what is understood as legitimate knowledge production (Bullough & Pinnegar, 2001) and has challenged me to reconsider where power structures exist and how I can push back against them. Self-study draws attention to the impossibility of objective social research because "who the researcher is, is central to what the researcher does" (p. 13). Samaras (2011) emphasizes that self-study research is mediated in multiple confluences whereby "self-study is individual and collective, personal and interpersonal, and private and public" (p. 70). According to Bullough and Pinnegar (2001) "quality self-study research requires that a researcher negotiate a particularly sensitive balance between biography and history" (p. 15). Self-study is not simply a focus on the self as the name suggests, rather self-study is a focus on the intersection between the self and the practice (Mooney, 1957; Samaras, 2011; Bullough & Pinnegar, 2001).

Throughout the research process, the autobiographical and narrative nature of the self-study emerged through a framework in the same spirit as Samaras et al. (2004) which they define as personal history self-study. They suggest that

> Through a personal history self-study approach, professors and their students are able to reconstruct significant life events to inform them of their professional identity formation and to help them make meaning of their pedagogy and the connections of their practice to theory. (pp. 905-906)

Personal history self-study, which I identify as critical personal history self-study, allowed for an emphasis and paradigmatical recognition that we always bring who we are into the school and the classroom—the total of our affective explicit and implicit life experiences. The entangled nature of self and history is foundational to the self-study process. Accordingly, Britzman (1986) shares that investigating self and history

> Allows the individual critical insight into both the nature of her/his relationship to individuals, institutions, cultural values, and political events, and the ways in which these social relationships contribute to the individuals' identity, values, and ideological perspectives. In this way, individuals do have the capacity to participate in shaping and responding to the social forces which directly affect their lives. (p. 452)

In a similar manner, Samaras et al. (2004) posit "who we are as people, affects who we are as teachers and consequently our students' learning" (p. 906).

The bricolage of research methodologies and methods has enabled the bringing-to-light of one school teacher-turned-administrator's educative life journey. Themes and pathways that emerged through the reflexive critical personal history self-study research process has afforded for identity formation and confirmation within the confluence of outwardly appearing contradictory paradigms of teaching and learning. By revisioning the tensions of contradictory paradigms through alternative vantage points, hopeful opportunities to foster generative and transformative possibilities of teaching paradigms surfaced.

Participants

Because this is a personal history self-study, I was the primary participant. However, nothing is ever that simple. My personal recollections, narratives, and dialogical experiences are rooted in enmeshed social interactions and interpretations. I brought with me not just non-linear remembrances of past moments, but also the emotions, reactions, and relationality that I connect and associate to people, place, and time. Who and what I recall was intimately interwoven within my conscious and unconscious, drawn out through occasionally troubling dialogical, narrative, and written activities. The many dialogical moments afforded through the self-study have illuminated my incompleteness as a person, partner, father, community member, and educator. The study has afforded for "a diffuse revisioning of the past through the lens of the present in tension with another—that allows us to reconstruct our memories and thoughts" (Markides & Miller, 2018, p. 150).

Data Collection and Analysis

The participant in this critical personal history self-study is the researcher—me—who also happens to be a teacher-turned-school-administrator. Through the data collection and analysis process, data collected/witnessed/written as part of the study was made public to critical friends. It is the publicizing of reflective data that leads "to another series of processes that need to reside outside the individual… and move to wider communication and consideration of ideas, i.e., the generation and communication of new knowledge and understanding" (Loughran & Northfield, 1998, p. 15).

The interpretation of the study's findings focused on emergent possibilities. In this context—a divergence from positivism—there were no outliers because of the value being placed on a diversity of stories. Through this lens, diversity is understood to increase the robustness of research. There was no intention for generalizability within the study, in fact Holt-Reynolds (1991) suggests that one of the purposes of personal history self-study is to move away from generalizability towards contextual understandings.

> It is not reasonable to expect that every conclusion based on the personal experiences of one individual will be appropriate to generalize to all students. Some of the beliefs that… teachers bring to their study of teaching will, in fact, be based on insufficient data and will, therefore, be invalid for generalizing to larger groups of students— Changing, challenging, enlarging, informing, and reforming the premises upon which… teachers base their arguments become our primary and legitimate concerns. (p. 21)

It is important to understand that through the generative sharing of personal stories regarding educational experiences and professional learning I hoped that I better understand my possible impacts on teaching paradigms and students' learning. However, measuring the direct impact of administrators' work on student learning outcomes was not addressed within this study; instead, how one administrator felt that the divergent possibilities afforded through disruptive learning experiences could challenge embodied hegemonic positivistic paradigms of teachers was a major consideration.

Continued and Emergent Positioning: Researcher Assumptions

Throughout this section I continue to position myself. I further share my beliefs, understandings, and assumptions regarding education in Alberta and how these assumptions influence what I have come to understand about the work and pedagogies of school administrators as it pertains to the study. Throughout the following sections I refer to educators or administrators; I referred to them in the context of educators in Alberta, even though readers may possibly make connections to all education (early childhood elementary, secondary, post-secondary, etc.).

I have come to this place—the moment where I am today as the sum of my lived history through an infinitude of interactions—by way of a strict objectivist, rationalist, axiom-based, North American scientific paradigm, the only correct paradigm that my Western Canadian schooling allows. My interpretive lens came from my socialized, negative-feedback-focused sense of self, and the understandings I have been conditioned into from my own schooling experience. When I refer to this moment, I am referring to the current location where I am as both a space and feeling. I share these thoughts because it is important to establish *relational accountability* (Wilson, 2008; Kovach, 2017) as an affordance of *relational trust* (Robinson, 2011) before I look to disrupt pre-established truths.[9]

Britzman (2003) contends that contemporary educators are effectively indoctrinated members of one of the most familiar professions in Canadian culture. Teachers currently in schools have existed, and likely functioned well or found success within the contexts of education throughout most of their lives. As the result of extensive, insular, and similar experiences of schooling, pedagogical understandings of what schooling and education *are*, likely deeply paradigmatically entrenched, many teachers (re)enact or appropriate their lived experiences within classrooms. As a result, opening possibilities to transformative pedagogies require a level of reflexivity that may be afforded through disruptive professional learning—learning that makes the familiar strange (Davis et al., 2015).

Transformations and reconsiderations of educator paradigms can come through disruptive professional learning opportunities that challenge their recalled memories of pedagogical experiences through new generative dialogical experiences. Kanu and Glor (2006) advocate that transforming professional practice "requires scepticism towards all of one's educational experience" (p.

103). Tentatively-held paradigms will allow for the divergence of pedagogical practices, practice which may subsume those of their past and evolve to incorporate openness to a multiplicity of epistemologies. Through the reflexive (re)consideration of the possibilities that may be afforded through considering school and schooling as place, educators can act as individual change agents within the collective ecology of the school, schooling, culture,[10] curricula, and education.

Having grown up in Northern British Columbia, I feel a strong connection to land and nature. As a result, I understand the human/more-than-human (Abram, 1996) dichotomy to be false; instead, I view humans to be inseparable from the complexities and entangled interactions of both the biotic and abiotic. From my high school and post-secondary schooling experiences, which focused on Newtonian and Cartesian positivistic, cause-effect understandings of education and specifically mathematics and physics, I feel the need to "correctly" and objectively predict and prove new understandings as disembodied from the world. Throughout my teaching career I have worked to reconcile these understandings of the world and have been troubled by the impact that these beliefs could have on the students entrusted to my care. I work to ensure that I am not perpetuating a division between students' lived understandings of the world and their classroom experiences (Seidel, 2014). Through these tensions I have come to see that "the world is not an aggregation of things, but rather a symphony of relationships between many participants that are altered by the interaction" (Weber, 2017, p. 30); and, I desire to provoke such hopefulness with students.

I am an educator-turned-administrator, and in this role, I occasionally feel that I have been disempowered of my teaching voice with colleagues, while being empowered in an authoritative capacity. I am now responsible for a large community of staff and students. I am accountable to a parent council, to a divisional board of trustees, and to an executive team who expects statistics supporting school improvement indicators. As a result of these accountabilities and responsibilities, I feel the pressure to support change within the school while recognizing an informal inherited curriculum (Tarc, 2011) passed down through generations of teachers since the conception of formalized education.

How will I foster change within my school and schooling context? How can I disrupt the hegemonic narrative of convergent absolutist pedagogical understandings? How will I ethically act as a change agent within the school community? How can I help to facilitate an understanding of school as a place that embodies the pedagogies of hope, love, trust, humility, and relationality?

How can I support educators in understanding that fostering relationships between and amongst curriculum, the human, and more-than-human is vital to an ancillary emergence of possibilities?

Limitations and Delimitations

It is important that I explicitly state the limitations and delimitations as I understood them for this self-study (Bloomberg & Volpe, 2016). By bringing what I understood as limitations and delimitations unapologetically into explicit dialogue, I continue to reflexively unpack and share my emergent paradigm and biases.

The most prominent limitation of this study was the set of biases which I brought with my affective experiences, viewed, and envisioned through my only lens—my current one. Through self-study I hoped to know myself better outside of myself. Through my positionings I attempted to both implicitly and explicitly share some of my biases. I hope to have articulated that I understood my educational life to exist within the tension of what I believe to be the prominent Western Canadian, positivist, reductionist, isolated, static hegemonic paradigm of schooling and the reality of life that is social, collective, emergent, complex and in constant flux. I understand effective education to be (inter/intra)connected and relational, wholistic, and entangled, and I know effectively implemented curriculum embodied in a similar manner.

I understand that an additional limitation of this study was the subjectivity associated with the analysis of data. The analysis of data in this project was affected by my own subjectivity. To address this subjectivity, I recursively engaged in dialogue with critical friends as suggested by Samaras (2011) which served to critique and disrupt understandings and knowledges which I previously held onto with certainty. As mentioned earlier, there was no intention within the context of this study to generalize the findings. However, it is important to recognize that there will always be a certain degree of transferability with all research (Bloomberg & Volpe, 2016) which may happen through the acts of reader interpretation and coherence making.

A delimitation to this study was the restriction of my own current contextual understandings of education enacted through Alberta Education's Program of Studies (Alberta Education, 2019). This was an intentional choice because most of my experiential knowledge has been formulated through working, living, and teaching in Alberta and Alberta accredited schools.

Additionally, I used the Foundational Principles of High School Redesign (Alberta Education, 2018a) as a current representation of prominent high school pedagogical intention within Alberta. It is important to note that I understand the responsibilities and requirements on and of school administrators to be highly contextual and evolutionary (Bedard & Mombourquette, 2015), and often require different enactments and understandings than other grade configurations. Another delimitation of the research could be considered due to the small sample size; this was intentional as it is the point of personal history self-study. I believe that more descriptive and personalized data afforded more contextualized and interconnected data (Merriam, 2009).

Summary

Chapter One provided a brief overview of the context and intention of this research study including context, positioning, research problem, purpose, theoretical framework, significance, research questions, methodology, limitations and delimitations, and definition of terms. In Chapter Two, an extensive literature review examining current research and their historical lineages focusing on the areas of the Foundational Principles of High School Redesign (Alberta Education, 2018a), metaphor theory, teacher and administrator metaphorical understandings, prominent Western Canadian metaphorical understandings of education, alternative and critical pedagogies, and ecological sensibilities as relevant to education was undertaken. From this investigation, I share that the shifting in leadership and teaching responsibilities as outlined by Bedard and Mombourquette (2015), and Alberta Education (2018a) is an evolutionary and complex undertaking. Supported through effective and visionary leadership the evolution of teaching pedagogies from reductionist, positivist, schooling towards enmeshed ecological sensibilities and pedagogical possibilities of hope and love may be possible. Chapter Three details the explicitly addressed theoretical framework that grounded this study as well as methodologies, ethical considerations, data collection methods, and research settings will be discussed at length

Notes

1 According to Varela et al. (2016) an enactment is the bringing forward of meaning from background understanding. This was an idea originating from the work of Maturana and

Varela (1987). According to Davis, Sumara, and Luce-Kapler (2018), an enactment is the bringing forward of "tacit knowledge [that] is simply knitted into one's being" (p. 85).

2 Embody or embodying refers to the outward physical and visible observable characteristics of a typically inward idea or concept. Literally it means to bring to the body.

3 The process of becoming is a recognition of the tentative nature of my identity as an educator—one which is never complete and always in flux. This identity, as described by Britzman (2003), comes from my recursive revisitation to childhood understandings of the familiar profession of teaching through my new and emergent lens as an educator. The process of becoming is the acknowledgment of the co-evolution of my teaching identity and the impact that teaching has on me.

4 I use the term wholistic in the spirit of Leroy Little Bear's (2000) *wholeness*, whereby he suggests:

wholeness speaks to the totality of creation, the group as opposed to the individual…. It focuses on the totality of the constant flux rather than on individual patterns…. Wholeness is like a flower with four petals. When it opens, one discovers strength, sharing, honesty, and kindness. Together these four petals create balance, harmony, and beauty. Wholeness works in the same interconnected way. (p. 79)

5 I understand personal history self-study in a similar manner to Sumaras (2010) and Samaras, Hicks, and Garvey Berger (2004) whereby I situate myself within the field of education and reflexively and recursively consider how I have come to understand myself and my identity. Through the support of critical friends, I critically interrogate my previously held understandings. See personal history self-study in Chapter Three for more clarity.

6 I use the term positioning as a reference to me sharing myself and who I understand me to be with readers. It is important that readers know who I am so that they may better understand my paradigm and in turn, my intentions.

7 I use the term Albertan education to represent my understanding of a reductionistic fact-focused *banking model* of education (Freire, 1996), one which understands student knowledge to be in a state of deficit until properly filled up in an appropriate manner. I am hesitant to use generalizations such as North American or Western Education even though the terms may be applicable in this context. I will occasionally use the term Western Canadian because of my personal context. Nisbett (2003) identifies Western education to be linked to the teachings of the Greeks: focusing on logical axiomatically-based scientific pedagogies, scientific method, and rationality, which are in contrast with (intra/inter)connected Confucian rooted Eastern pedagogies of Japan, Korea. and China.

8 I use the words evolution, evolve, or evolutionary throughout my writing. I use the term cautiously because, as with all language, these terms can carry with them negative connotations and misinterpretations. I chose these terms intentionally and align my understandings with those of Davis et al. (2008, 2015) and Davis (2009) whereby evolution is a transformation over time and not a perpetuation of Social Darwinism. I want to challenge the disconnected social Darwinian "survival of the fittest" rhetoric in a similar manner to Youngblood (2000), Saul (2014), and Davis (2009) as it is being applied to education through my writing.

9 While this research is situated in the past act of writing this book, my use of the present tense as to location, space and feeling indicates my continued present.
10 Culture, in this case, refers to the way that Davis (2009) describes culture as the entirety of language, religion, artifacts, and beliefs that may come as part of a collective communal knowledge system. These are inseparably entangled. Additionally, Cruikshank (2000) defines culture "as a uniquely human creation central to everyday lives and practices of all human communities and characterized by our capacity to endow the world with symbolic meaning" (p. 1). Little Bear (2000) suggests that "culture comprises a society's philosophy about the nature of reality, the values that flow from this philosophy, and the social customs that embody these values" (p. 77).

· 2 ·

SELF-STUDY AND LITERATURE

In order to delve into educators' and administrators' understandings of prominent Western Canadian metaphors of education, I endeavoured to provide a glimpse of the evolving understandings of the following: leadership frameworks within the context of Alberta; self-study; metaphor theory and prominent Western Canadian metaphors for education; complexity and ecological pedagogical sensibilities; and critical pedagogies and critical and emergent possibilities for educational leadership. Definitions of metaphor, metaphor theory, educational paradigms are explored through the critical lens of an educator, administrator, parent, and student, while a focus on critical pedagogies of love is considered for alternative possibilities for education and leadership.

Selection Criteria: A review of scholarly resources: books, peer-reviewed research articles, and reports published via educational organizations was conducted. The selection criteria were as follows:

- A cross-section of research containing qualitative methodologies.
- Research based on Canadian context and specifically Albertan context was prioritized for the consideration of leadership; however, when considering metaphor theory, complexity, pedagogies of love, ecological sensibilities, and critical theory and pedagogies international research

- articles, books, and reports were not excluded if relevance to the topic was current.
- Contemporaneous literature was given top priority; however, gaps in the literature did require the inclusion of older material from the research field.
- Older seminal research was included to support a lineage of thought and understanding of relevant research topics.
- Non-peer review scholarship has been considered throughout this literature review and was selected based on whom the authors were referencing and who had referenced their work. This work has been intentionally chosen to support the voice of stakeholders whose voices may be missed through a strictly peer-reviewed authorship.

Search Procedure: Between September 2018 through December 2020, a search for peer-reviewed work was undertaken using the following key words and phrases: *Leadership in Alberta, Alberta Leadership Quality Standard, impacts of leadership competencies, instructional leadership, transformational and regenerative leadership, complexity and education, metaphor theory, prominent Western, Western Canadian, and North American metaphors for education, ecological sensibilities and education, critical pedagogies, pedagogies of hope and love, love, radical listening*. Search strategies utilized during this time included:

- Electronic searches on the following databases: Google Scholar, ProQuest, and ERIC.
- Regular and ongoing internet searches using Google.
- Recommendations from prominent scholars in relevant fields.
- Limited manual searches of scholarly texts found at the University of Calgary.

The following literature review considers a wide variety of references and resources, the relevance of which will prove to be valuable through the consideration of the wholeness of the work. It is my hope that readers will be not only informed through the sum of the review but moved to consider alternative possibilities as the result of its contemplations.

Introduction

The purpose of this research is to illuminate alternative possibilities for Albertan primary and secondary education that may serve to disrupt current rationalist, reductionist pedagogies and paradigms that are perpetuated by top-down expectations and associated popular literatures. Uncovering my own presently-held understandings helps to focus on areas where I have and may continue to transcend these currently held metaphors of education. A goal of this research was to better know myself through personal history self-study. Ultimately my goal was to provide the personal "opportunity to disrobe, unveil, and engage in a soul-searching truth about the self while also engaging in critical conversations, and most importantly, continuing to discover the alternative viewpoints of others" (Samaras et al., 2004, p. 910), with the anticipation of better understanding the evolution of my paradigm to that of divergent ecological sensibilities through a critically transformative lens evoking a pedagogy of love.

Through this literature review readers are asked to consider the new LQS, Teaching Quality Standards (TQS), and Foundational Principles of High School Redesign as possible "enabling constraints" (Davis et al., 2008, p. 193) for practicing educators and administrators. Historical metaphors and associated enacted practices are shared to better contextualize where education is currently within the Province of Alberta and to also lay groundwork for future possibilities within education in Alberta. Considerations of alternatives to prominent absolutist, rationalist, and positivist understandings of education such as ecological curricula with a specific focus on complexity and collectivity are brought forward and highlighted. Finally, through a consideration of the possibilities associated with critical pedagogy this literature review sets the foundation for the enactments of pedagogies of love as alternative possibilities for education in Alberta.

Throughout this literature review I made use of quotations from many prominent and diverse scholars. The use of extensive quotation as opposed to paraphrasing citation within a critical literature review was my chosen alternative to formal scholarship on literature reviews (see Bloomberg & Volpe, 2016; Ridley, 2012). As I looked to discuss alternative possibilities for education and leadership in Alberta, I also looked to disrupt the normative paradigms for the production of literature reviews by allowing the voices of the referenced scholars to be evident. It is my hope that through using quotations, I was able to "dialogue" with the many voices of the scholars, and in doing so share my positionality because you need to know significantly more about me before you can begin to understand my work (Wilson, 2008).

As I wrote and rewrote these words, I struggled to find a coherent vernacular to articulate my critical thoughts—thoughts that sought to challenge hegemonic education structures and beliefs. I grappled with the ways in which I understand the world—a world which I was confident was predictable and dependable; a paradigm that once worked for me, but is no longer adequate. The paradigm that served me well throughout my formal schooling is failing me. The holes in what I understand as truth are beginning to emerge. As I learn more and experience more, know better and take up knowledge in better ways, I struggle to find coherence with prior understandings. My paradigm is undergoing a radical, unsettling, and life-altering transformation. However, as I read and reread, I came to the realization that the only lens and paradigm that I can view and understand through is one which is deeply entrenched in the project which I struggle against. As I edited and challenged my own thoughts, I recognized that I may, in fact, be perpetuating the same binaries which I argue against. This was not my intention. I suggest that if there is language within the following work that seems to perpetuate a binary, I am hoping to perpetuate instead, a continuous dynamic spectrum. When I use language of *from* and *towards*, such as in Table 1, I do not intend for readers to envision discrete locations or times, rather a dynamic of possible change.

Changing Roles of Leadership

According to Leithwood (2012), "as our conception of district purposes shift from efficient administration of schools to key structures for facilitating school improvement, our understanding of the qualities of 'successful' districts has to change accordingly" (p. viii). The roles of school leaders have shifted drastically over the past decades from a role primarily focused on management towards one which now includes management but also includes instructional leadership (Fullan, 2012; Hallinger, 2010), community engagement (Deal, 2009; Knapp et al., 2010), and administrative mentorship (Honig, 2012; Honig, et al., 2010; Fullan, 2014; Whitaker, 2013; Muhammad, 2009; Marzano et al., 2011; Reeves, 2009). Table 1 illustrates how the roles of leadership have changed and continue to change for educational leaders.

Table 1. Shifts in Educational Leadership Through Time as Adapted from Bedard and Mombourquette (2015)

Shifts in Educational Leadership	
From	Towards
Compliance based	• Building on shared commitment and dignity (Hargreaves & Lowenhaupt, 2017) • Capacity building • Focus on mission and vision
Administrative matters and managerial work	• Instructional Leadership • Leveraging relationships • Culture building
Loosely connected divisional elements	• Tight alignment with articulated intention • Denser professional networks (Hargreaves & O'Connor, 2017, 2018)
Traditional, top-down decision making	• Sharing and collaborating of ideas (Hargreaves & Ainscow, 2015) • More permeable boundaries between district and schools
Narrow data collection	• Broader means and acceptance of data collection • Wider array of data used to support district and school initiatives
Leadership succession	• Focused, standards-based identification and selection
Outside, expert-based professional learning	• Embedded professional learning • Professional Learning Communities (PLC) (Hargreaves & O'Connor, 2017, 2018) • Increased leadership autonomy over school professional learning (Hargreaves & Lowenhaupt, 2017)
Passive engagement of stakeholders	• Building productive stakeholder relationships • Consulting with stakeholders • Building relational trust (Robinson, 2011) • Increasing transparency

The prominent changes that stand out in the righthand column in Table 1 allude to the understandings that engagement of community and collectivity are recognized to be drastically more important than they were in the past. Considerations of stakeholder input, consultation, and trust is recognized as a priority (Deal, 2009; Honig et al., 2010). Additionally, there is a new understanding that education and school social responsibilities no longer end when the school day finishes or where the school property ends (Province of Alberta, 2018). Definitions of leadership in the context of schools have broadened to include alignment with district policy, mentorship of new and upcoming inductees and seamlessly incorporating the Foundational Principles of High School Redesign (Alberta Education, 2018a). Ultimately, leadership is now, more than ever, pedagogical responsibility—the art and science of modeling effective practice in relation to educators and learners (Anderson, 2018).

The foundational principles of high school redesign (Alberta Education, 2018a) and each of their indicators illustrate a shift in Alberta high schools' focus toward the affordances for student-centered leaning, choice, and flexibility. The foundational principles include an increased focus on mastery learning, rigorous and relevant curriculum, flexible learning environments, educator roles and professional development, meaningful relationships, home and community involvement, assessment, and welcoming, caring, respectful, and safe learning environments (Alberta Education, 2018a). The specifics of each of these principles have been implicitly subsumed into the new Alberta Teaching Quality Standard and the Leadership Quality Standard; however, reading the documents as separate and in parallel helps to emphasize the subtle differences in age-specific pedagogies.

The principles listed above are not intended to be additional to the changing roles of education but are intended to be interconnected as part of changing and responsive pedagogies. According to Alberta Education (2018a) high school redesign is "focused on three outcomes: engaged students, high levels of achievement and quality teaching. It's about redesigning high school to be more student-centred and responsive" (para. 1). These shifts are fundamental to increasing opportunity for all students' success as shared in the following reference:

High School Redesign is about more than simply shifting a timetable. It's about shifting mindsets. While the timetable shift opens the door for schools to create flexible learning environments, the mindset shift leads to changes in practice that ensure the flexible learning environments are used to support increased student engagement in learning, improved student achievement and enhanced teacher practice. (Alberta Education, 2018a, para. 2)

According to Friesen et al. (2015), Alberta high schools that have been successful in transforming educational paradigms within their collective contexts all share similar characteristics relative to the Foundational Principles of High School Redesign. See Table 2 below for the findings and recommendations for schools, principals, and district leaders for the effective enactment of the High School Redesign that "provide a deeper understanding of the conditions that impact iterative change and the leadership and pedagogy required to create adaptive learning systems in high schools" (p. 5).

Table 2. Findings (actions required) and Recommendations (for increasing adaptive learning capacity) of and for Effective High School Redesign Implementation as Adapted from Friesen et al. (2015)

Schools	
Findings	Recommendations
Changing structures to support a learner focus	Remove structures such as a 25-hour credit requirement for all learners.
Focus on growth-orientation, risk-taking attitudes, and actions. Support community, and peer connection	
Focus on collaborative inquiry	Learning systems need a collaborative inquiry approach to design
Increase an emphasis on visible teaching including mentorship and feedback	Learning systems need visible teaching.
An increased focus on vertical and horizontal understandings of curriculum. Across content areas	Learning systems require a comprehensive understanding of curriculum and assessment.
Student voice must be incorporated as part of ongoing feedback.	Learning systems need to regularly seek input from students and other school and system level influences.

Principals	
Findings	Recommendations
Professional learning should focus on student learning and work to improve student outcomes.	Ongoing, continuous professional learning focused on student learning is required throughout the learning system for leaders and teachers; learning systems need to have high expectations for all learners.
Educator collective leadership and responsibility in the implementation of data-informed and research-based professional learning using cycles of inquiry.	Learning systems require a collective, design-based orientation to leadership guided by a theory of action for change.
Diversification of student and teacher success indicators of success.	School leaders need to continually use data-informed, research-based, multiple indicators of success as evidence to inform iterative changes during cycles of inquiry.
District Leaders	
Findings	Recommendations
Affordances for the characteristics of highly adaptive and complex learning systems	All levels within learning systems need highly adaptive networks of school and system level influences guided by a theory of action for change.
Varied levels of connection for principals' learning support from the district level.	

In the next section, I consider how metaphors and metaphorical understandings held by teachers and educational leaders not only impact the way that they view the world but are also telling as to their beliefs about learning and learners. It is my hope that through the reflexive consideration of prominent metaphorical understandings in education and their entailments, educators may be able to broaden their beliefs regarding the possibilities of education. I am suggesting that through a deeper, more dynamic awareness of personal metaphors of teaching we may be able to shift pedagogies from those of the "impossible imperative assignment" (Markides, 2018, p. 42). Through introspection and a reflexive consideration of teaching identity (Lyle, 2017) the impossible may disappear and may become the mindful enactment of educators working collectively to make a real change (Markides, 2018). Put differently, educators and educational leaders, through the consideration of a multiplicity of educational metaphors "are being asked to consider identity not so much as something already present, but rather as production, in the throes of being constituted as we live in places of difference" (Aoki, 1993, p. 260).

Metaphors and Metaphorical Understandings

Metaphor Theory is grounded in the work of George Lakoff and Mark Johnson (Lakoff & Johnson, 1980; Lakoff & Johnson, 1999; Johnson, 1987; Lakoff, 1993), whereby they suggest, "metaphors constitute the universe of abstract ideas, that they create rather than reflect it, that they are the source of our understandings, imagination, and reasoning" (Sfard, 1994, p. 47). According to this theory, humans subconsciously incorporate metaphors and think through them in their dialogue "whenever people talk about topics that are even slightly abstract or complex" (Gereluk et al., 2016, p. 42). Metaphor theory was initially proposed as an alternative to objectivism during the 1960s and 1970s and has since been adopted as the prominent theory, displacing objectivism, as the commonly held belief around knowing and learning.

Objectivism is grounded in the belief that meaning is disembodied from the human mind (Sfard, 1994), and in that context "understanding is conceived as 'grasping the meaning' and thus as a process which mediates between an individual mind and the universally experienced, absolute, ahistorical realm of facts and idea" (p. 45). Objectivism is steeped in humanistic beliefs of *a* singular affective experience which makes possible disembodied understandings of meaning—meanings which are axiomatically assumed to be universal and implicitly understood through language (Gereluk et al., 2016; Sfard, 1994). According to this paradigm, knowing means to represent accurately what is outside of the mind, inside the head (Rorty, 1979). Davis et al. (2008) suggest that objectivism is axiomatic of a mentalist paradigm "that rel[ies] on the premise that learning is a matter of building an internal model or representation of an external reality" (p. 96). Through this paradigm increased clarity through explanation would be the necessary change for acquisition of understanding.

Lakoff and Johnson (1980) challenge objectivist understandings of learning with the alternative understandings of the now widely accepted Metaphor Theory. Schön (1993) proposes that metaphor "refers both to a certain kind of product—a perspective or frame, a way of looking at things—and to a certain kind of process—a process by which new perspectives on the world come into existence" (p. 137). Often the idea of metaphor is strictly considered from the lens of figurative language; however, Lakoff (1993) suggests that there cannot be a division between the literal and figurative language. He claims that "the locus of metaphor is thought, not language, that metaphor is a major and indispensable part of our ordinary, conventional way of conceptualizing the world, and that our everyday behavior reflects our metaphorical understanding of experience" (p. 204). These are profound statements when considered through the ways that teachers may enact their beliefs about students and learning. Lakoff (1993) goes on to suggest that metaphor is a coherence-making exercise that is enacted "in the way that we conceptualize one mental domain in terms of another" (p. 203).

In the following section, I present specific examples of what metaphors are in terms of learning and knowing. I continue by discussing how the metaphors that educators and administrators hold, if not held in a tacit and subsumable manner may lead to an irreconcilability when faced with alternative schemas or emergent situations.

Reification as Emergent Possibility

Lakoff (1993) suggests that there may be examples where we can take our experiences to be literal, for example "the balloon went up" (p. 205), however as soon as we move from the concrete to the physical all experiences become metaphorical. Which is precisely why metaphor and the understandings of metaphors in teaching is crucial, because the acts of teaching are inherently abstract (Munby, 1986). Even something as seemingly simple as the counting of numbers becomes part of the realm of metaphors for both educators and learners because of the possible incongruence between the symbolic representation of the number itself or the number as a quantity (Davis & Renert, 2013a, 2013b; Lakoff & Nunez, 2000).

Making sense of the complexity of feelings and experiences is the antithesis of common rationalist understandings. It is precisely the incommensurability of the aforementioned which has challenged cognitive researchers to develop alternative theories to understand how we learn—challenging the perpetuation of the Cartesian dualistic belief of the mind separate from the body. It is important to recognize that this dualism is not a prominent understanding in Eastern philosophy (Nesbitt, 2003). Lakoff and Johnson (1980, 1999) have challenged the Objectivist conception of cognition by disproving this dualism. They suggest that "our bodily experience is the main—in fact the only—source of understanding" (Sfard, 1994, p. 46). When we engage with ideas that are even remotely complex or abstract, we engage in what is known as an *ontological mapping* (Lakoff, 1993), which is the beginning of a process of sense-making. We look to take two seemingly distinct or independent ideas or *conceptual domains* (Lakoff, 1993) and consider the ideas through a metaphorical mapping that may help us to better grasp the experience.

If we take the idea of *love*, for example, which is inherently abstract and challenging to define, we can apply a metaphor of love as/is a journey. According to Lakoff (1993) the *love as a journey* metaphor is not simply words:

> It is the ontological mapping across conceptual domains, from the source domain of journeys to the target domain of love. The metaphor is not just a matter of language, but of thought and reason. The language is secondary. The mapping is primary, in that it sanctions the use of source domain language and inference patterns for target domain concepts. The mapping is conventional; that is, it is a fixed part of our conceptual system, one of our conventional ways of conceptualizing love relationships. (p. 208)

This is one particular metaphor; I suggest that within the context of education we would struggle to find a concept, process, or understanding that we wouldn't engage with metaphorically. An example: how do we discuss time? We consider it to be a quantity or a measurement, but it is never simply a disembodied thing. We speak of running out of time or wasting time. When we look at operations in mathematics and consider multiplication, we would struggle not to define the concept in terms of actions or other experiences: multiplication as stretching, or groups of, or scaling (Markides & Miller, 2018; Davis & Renert, 2013a, 2013b; Lakoff & Nunez, 2000). What about our understandings of reading, writing, communicating, learning, knowing, etc.? None of these examples can be considered simple. The abstractions, embodiments, and experiences associated with any of these would be as varied as the affective experiences of the person enacting them.

Lakoff and Johnson (1980) suggest that it is through a sense-making metaphorical construction that we work to find coherence within our *embodied schema*. Johnson (1987) defines a schema as "structures *of an activity* by which we organize experience in ways that we can comprehend. They are primary means by which we *construct or constitute* order and are not mere passive receptacles into which experience is poured" (pp. 29-30). These embodied schemas, in the context of learning can create an incoherence or logical break if or when they are no longer subsumable in each context (see Markides & Miller, 2018). However, when taken up in an appropriate manner the ontological mapping from source domains (Journey) to target domains (Love) may afford for the reification of abstract or complex ideas towards understandings.

Metaphors of Schooling and Associated Practices

The consideration of metaphors and metaphor theory is of the utmost importance when discussing education because education, according to Britzman (2003, 2013), is the *impossible task*. It is this impossible task which requires educators to continually challenge what they believe about students and learning. (Austin, 1996; Bullough & Stokes, 1994). Weber and Mitchell (1995) suggest that it is "how people think about teaching may be shaped in many ways by the images of teacher in popular culture that they encounter in their daily lives" (p. 20). Education and the associated acts, choices, and pedagogies are all the embodiments of teachers' experiences, beliefs, metaphors, and schema (Gereluk et al., 2016; Allbritton, 1995; Munby, 1986), whether intentional or subconscious that are used to "understand abstract concepts and to organize our thinking about them" (Gereluk et al., 2016, p. 44). As a result, it would be logical to suggest that there is a direct positive correlation between the complexity of a concept and the necessary diversity of associated metaphors (Gereluk et al., 2016).

According to Gereluk et al. (2016) there are three prominent metaphors associated with Albertan education: "teaching as building, learning as development, and teaching as guiding" (p. 44). The previously stated scholars draw on the work of Lakoff and Johnson (1980) and Davis (2004) to suggest that each of the three metaphors can be directly linked to specific conceptualizations, enactments, and associated prominent pedagogies, see Table 3.

Table 3. Prominent Metaphors and Associated Affordances Adapted from Gereluk et al. (2016); Entailments Related to Metaphors (Davis & Renert, 2013a, 2013b)

		Entailments	
Prominent Metaphors and Connections to Fundamental Movements in Teaching	Conceptualizations of Teaching	Associated Metaphors; Teaching as:	Associated Metaphors; Learning as:
Teaching as Building • Constructionism • Platonism • Science Driven Teaching • Enlightenment • Banking models of education (Freire, 1996) • Educational Rationalism	• Focused on systematic bodies of knowledge • Simplicity (Weaver, 1948) • A singular truth • Clarity of explanation is directly correlated and positively to learner understandings	• construction • planned/structured and predictable • following a predetermined pathway (Bovitch, Cullimore, Bramwell-Jones, Massas, & Perun, 2011). • instruction	• acquiring • mechanistic building • building on basic/foundational knowledge
Teaching as Guiding • Discovery learning • Discrepancies between Eastern and Western beliefs about education (Nesbitt, 2003)	• Truths exist "out there" in the world	• supporting in gaining wisdom • leading towards personal potential/development	• (Re)discovering lost knowledge • A means to function well in the world • recollection
Learning as Development • Ecological sensibilities • Organic metaphors • Piagetian Constructivism • Socio-Constructivism • Recognition of Complexity of interaction • University-based • Brain-based	• Competency-based • Evolution of understandings	• creator of favourable conditions for learning • disruptor of previously held schema • drawing out • critical thinking (Chomsky, 1999) • supporting happiness (Noddings, 2004) • supporting self-esteem (Emler, 2001) • supporting self-realization (Rogers, 1995)	• changes in cognition through lived experience • an evolutionary process • curiosity • understanding relation to the environment • connections to the social world

While there is a chronological linearity to the popularity and usage of each of these prominent metaphors, their current enactments are by no means discretely enacted. In fact, there are many instances where teachers unknowingly draw from multiple prominent educational metaphors. The reason why it is imperative to consider which metaphors administrators and teachers hold and embody for education and learning is because Gereluk et al. (2016) suggest "there is a relationship between the metaphors people use when they talk about a particular topic and their beliefs about that topic. And by influencing our thinking, metaphors can affect our choices" (p. 44). It is precisely these choices and the associated beliefs that I wish to investigate through this self-study. By the investigation of metaphors associated with administrators' beliefs around their impact on disruptive teacher professional learning through self-study I hope to elicit a focused reflexivity around metaphorical entailments. Through broad contextual experiences and reflexive engagement, I hope that all educators: teachers, administrators, executive teams, trustees, etc. would continue to grow in their understandings of the complexities that are teaching and learning—the understanding that "the search for a single 'right' metaphor for education will almost always lead to an oversimplified, truncated conception of teaching and learning" (Gereluk et al., 2016, p. 59).

A Multiplicity of Metaphors

One of the lingering influences of rational and reductionistic teaching paradigms are dichotomous and hierarchical languages. As the result of our Western Canadian affective experiences, we fall into the trap of assuming that there can always be the best means to proceed or way to know, while there may be cases of situational simplicity (Weaver, 1948)—rigidly structured physical science-based experimentation. In these cases where there are little or no social influences or considerations there may well be the best way at that moment. However, in situations, specifically those of educational pragmatics where social interactions, cultural nuances, and situational constructs are legitimate influences, rarely will there be a single correct answer, response, or direction. In fact, due to a multiplicity of world curricula (Lessard et al., 2015; Aoki, 1993, 2004) there may well be an infinitude of possible interpretations, or understandings associated with any one situation. As Gereluk et al. (2016) suggest:

> No single metaphor is up to the task of capturing the many faces of teaching, and none of the corresponding conceptions of teaching and learning that can be associated with the dominant metaphors of education can fully capture teaching's complex and multifaceted nature. (p. 59)

According to Cook-Sather (2003) there are several reasons to support a reflexive investigation and dialogue around educational metaphors. She suggests that through opening up to competing educational metaphors and paradigms educators will begin to understand that there are limitations to all metaphors. Additionally, as Gereluk et al. (2016) suggests, through a broader understanding of the prominent educational metaphors and their entailments educators will better understand that "the first step towards wisdom in teaching, then, may be to admit that good teaching will never be a simple matter" (p. 60).

Disrupting Paradigms: Towards A (Inter/Intra)-Connected Curriculum

Proponents of the safety of an absolutist and positivistic paradigm of education would perpetuate that education, when enacted in the *best* way, is predictable and controllable. However, when we consider the educational possibilities afforded through a connected paradigm, Doll (1993) suggests that "it is not the individual as an isolated entity which is important but the person within the communal, environmental frame. In fact, the concept of isolated or rugged individualism… is a fiction" (p. 92). A messy interconnected and collective understanding of education, learning, and learners may be a more adequate paradigm for the possibilities associated with the multiplicity of cultures, beliefs, and understandings that a social, interactive, (inter/intra)-connected humanity as a whole embodies. The wants and desires and the successes and failures of each society are as diverse as our planet's ecosystems, and no one way to exist can be considered the hierarchical best way.

Positivism and absolutism permeating current educational paradigms

I assume there would be a general claim that education has moved away from a Ralph Tyler model (Tyler, 1949) of education[1] towards one which is more appropriate, ethical, and accountable for today. However, the language, metaphors, and *entailments* (Davis & Renert, 2013a, 2013b) associated with positivistic conceptions of learning and accountability still hold sacrosanct influence over many current educational pedagogies.

bell hooks (1993) emphatically suggests that we need to "acknowledge that the education most of us had received and were giving was not and is never politically neutral" (p. 30). Through a Western Canadian lens of education there is *an* objective truth, *an* appropriate way to understand, and *an* acceptable way to show mastery of knowledge—a correct way to be educated. Effective educational improvement when considered through a positivistic lens is benchmarked through increased measurability, accountability, reproducibility, and efficiency (Giroux, 1997). Dei and Simmons (2018) share that:

> schooling and education have emerged as commodities of Enlightenment..., whereby the immanent cultural expressions, attitudes, and ways of behaving help to form the material conditions of the Eurosubject, as reified through the Western text. (p. 58)

As Doll (1993) suggests, through this lens, "we define good teaching (resulting in good learning) as the transfer of knowledge—often in the form of the noble works and accepted procedures of Western... tradition" (p. 58). With this view of education, learning is a linear, disconnected understanding of a reality that teaching authorities impose on less knowledgeable students.

Teachers engaging in a positivist paradigm often claim that they are preparing students for the real world (fictitious future) through the constructionistic building up or linear attainment of the correct knowledge, as is the goal and purpose of schooling (Gereluk et al., 2016). Using dualistic language, separating school and reality, teachers perpetuate a cause-effect singular pathway towards a successful future (Davis, 2004). In Chubberly's (1916) writing which feels as though it could have been written yesterday, it is suggested that "our schools are, in a sense, factories in which the raw products are to be shaped and fashioned into products to meet the various demands of life" (p. 338). Even micro-deviations from these prescribed paths must necessarily converge back to the appropriate path or they become an indicator of a knowledge deficit (Doll, 1993; Barto & Bedford, 2013). This singular pathway with a small margin of tolerance is the prescribed route set out by the dominant culture's hegemonic reality, leaving no room for difference.

The perception of a common experience lived inside and outside of school life, as perpetuated by Albertan education whose curriculum is time independent, certain, unchanging, and composed of objective truth, is not realistic (Lessard et al., 2015). The dualistic binaries of Descartes and Newton still propagate throughout schools where "knowledge [can] be discovered, but not created.... [as a result] we allow only one type of knowing: a rational, definitional knowing" (Doll, 1993, pp. 32-33). The idea that truth is out there or "detached rationalism is really the perspective of groups in society whose identities and experiences are considered to be the mythical norm" (Kumashiro, 2002, p. 76). But this detached rationalism is impossible.

Given the historical roots of Western Canadian education in The Enlightenment, industrialism, and rationalism, teachers have come by their pedagogical understandings honestly. The Tylerian rationale for a mechanistic pedagogy rooted in the logics of Descartes suggests that "classroom pedagogy does not question assumptions, beliefs, and paradoxes...; rather, it begins with what is self-evident or given and moves in linear links to reinforce, establish, or prove that already set and valued" (Doll, 1993, p. 115). While some teachers reading these lines may argue that we have moved away from these ideals, and others may believe that these are precisely the pedagogies which are the best and most effective, there can be no doubt that this type of dominating and oppressive language continues to persist in ways that perpetuate that "curriculum has been employed to neutralize difference" (Kanu, 2003, pp. 68-69). Through this paradigm where students-as-learners are often seen to be homogeneous within education and classrooms there is but one justifiable and logical understanding of reality—a dualistic superiority over others and a dominance over the environment.

Considering classrooms as complex adaptive systems

When one comes from a paradigm of control, there is a certain element of fear that exists with an inability to predict or control all aspects of what could happen in the classroom. According to Jones (2013) "to continue this next critical step in the evolution of educational thought will require educators to leave the comfort zone of our Cartesian and Newtonian perspective" (p. 818). Connected curricula and the associated pedagogies afford for the (re)imagining of education: an education that is inherently messy; an education that is occasionally uncomfortable; an education that is open, biological/ecological, and chaotic; an education that is meaningful, transformative, empowering, and hopefully emancipatory.

Through the consideration the classroom as a complex adaptive system we may begin to recognize the ancillary nature of teaching which may support the self-organizing, generative nature of learning (Schneider, & Somers, 2006)—environments where students with agency adapt and impact their own and all others' trajectories (Dewey, 2013, 1902; Wadlington, 2013). Embodying complex understandings of education could require paradigm shifts to recognize that the complexity of the classroom collective—complex relationships that are codependent and often bottom-up. In the context of classrooms as a complex adaptive system, Davis and Simmt (2006) suggest:

> a complex form is bottom-up; its emergence does not depend on central organizers or governing structures. As agents cohere into higher order unities, complex systems manifest transcendent properties and capacities that are not manifest among those individual agents. Because the "characters" of systems arise in co-specifying dynamics of agents, complex systems have a history. That is, they embody their experiences through continuous modifications in their relationships among agents. (pp. 295-296)

Shifts in paradigms will require everyone involved in education to begin to understand that "the future evolves from the present (and the past) and is dependent on the interactions that have happened and are continually happening.... Such a becoming process is determined but unpredictable" (Doll, 1993, p. 72). When considered through this alternative lens, Doll (1993) posits:

> The teaching-learning frame switches from a cause-effect one where learning is either a direct result of teaching or teaching is at least a superior-inferior relationship with learning. The switch is to a mode where teaching becomes ancillary to learning, with learning dominant, due to the individual's self-organizational abilities. (p. 101)

Additionally, Ellsworth (1997) shares:

> Pedagogy is a much messier and more inconclusive affair than the vast majority of our educational theories and practices make it out to be.... The pedagogical relation between student and teacher is a paradox. As a paradox, pedagogy poses problems and dilemmas that can never be settled or resolved once and for all. (p. 8)

Education considered through an (inter/intra)-connected context should consider the complexity that is associated with social interaction and a multiplicity of epistemologies—an education for all. Dei and Simmons (2018) suggest that:

> education for all must include the multiple ways we come to know and understand our social environment. Education for all must include the local everyday philosophies of students and all learners alike. We cannot continue to buy into the governing neo-liberal ideologies, which profess to be emancipatory and inclusive for all. (p. 58)

Through the consideration of classrooms as complex systems, educators may be able to support the engagement of all learners and begin to recognize that all students come into the space and place of the classroom with their own affective histories and experiences, each to be enacted through the context of that learning environment. In these redefined transformative spaces, administrators may support teacher understandings and pedagogies with a more emergent recognition for the possibilities of education. So, how do we as a collective of educators move towards this (inter/intra)-connected vision for education? How can administrators and teachers (co)support each other in shifting educational cultures by increasing their comfort around educational paradigms that recognize the potential unpredictability and messiness within a transformative curriculum?

In the next section I explore how opening the possibilities for ecological sensibilities for education through a critical lens may afford for a more wholistic education. The subsummation of the simplistic (Weaver, 1948), positivistic, and absolutist educational paradigms by those supporting the recognition of the complexities, multiplicities, influences, and attractors of social interactions can support all learners.

Moving from a Tylerian rationale towards Doll Jr's 4 R's, the (inter/intra)-connected, and ecological sensibilities

We are past the adequacy of a reductionistic, positivist driven application of the Tyler model (Tyler, 1949) of schooling that ignores community, treats students as interchangeable inputs, and reduces curriculum and student learning to an optimizable and predictable object. In 1918, Bobbitt (2013) stated, "the technique of the scientific method is at present being developed for every important aspect of education. Experimental laboratories and schools are discovering accurate methods of measuring and evaluating different types of educational processes" (p. 12). Bobbit went on to suggest that progress in education requires the replacement of prior models that were "mainly formulated during the simpler conditions of the nineteenth century… any inherited system, good for its time, when held to after its day, hampers social progress" (p. 11). By perpetuating social Darwinian representations reveals a de-historied and disconnected belief of control over the complexity of all social relationships, specifically in education.

Eisner (1997), in discussing the legitimacy of quantitative data, suggests that "not all forms of data representation have been considered legitimate in the context of research" (p. 5) which supported the intensive drive to quantify educational research data, and "is based on the fundamental misunderstanding of what education is about and a fundamental misunderstanding of what makes education 'work'" (Biesta, 2013, p. 3). As a result of this misrepresentation of the physical sciences, students and classrooms have been treated as variables. The associated data is disembodied and decontextualized as effect size measurements (see Hattie, 2011; Marzano, 2007) for the betterment of a fictitious, normative, "average" (Cohen, 2006) student. In this positivist context students are controllable and manipulate-able, having predictable, reproducible causal relationships with teaching. Educators need to be aware, cautious, and cognizant of the language that is inherited through previous iterations of curriculum and pedagogy—languages that perpetuate simplistic and reductionistic misconceptions of education through social Darwinian perspectives.

Within the context of traditional Albertan public schools and schooling, there have been few appropriate ways to know and act. As Banks (1980, as cited in Donald, 2016) states, "particular stories are selected as curricula because they have been deemed worth telling" (p. 12). This narrow margin of tolerable understanding and behavior comes from the hegemonic, oppressive, commonsense logics and is perpetuated through the repetition of schooling stories (Kumashiro, 2002). Teachers and administrators looking to broaden their understandings and paradigms regarding educational possibilities can begin by considering critical pedagogies and ecological sensibilities.

Steinberg and Kincheloe (2018) suggest that relationality can allow critical teachers to rethink classroom teaching and knowledges:

> Critical teachers can begin to understand the ecological base of our concept of relationality and the ways it can help us rethink classroom teaching and knowledge production. Monological forms of information produced in reductionistic disciplines are typically unconnected modes of knowledge alienated from other ways of knowing and being. (p. 36)

Education can be founded on paradigms of ecological sensibilities (Weber, 2017)—an ecology of living dynamic relationships where everything is co-implicit, co-impactful, and co-evolutionary. Students can be recognized as the individual change agents that they are, each with histories, cultures, and knowledges entangled within the collective community of learners. Education, as part of the complex dynamics of living relationships, creates room for disruption of what is already individually and collectively known, by *making the familiar strange* (Davis et al., 2015), and opening possibilities for epistemologies of hopeful imagination. By honoring and acknowledging learner differences as *enabling constraints* (Davis et al., 2008), rather than working to ignore, erase, or homogenize them, we acknowledge and celebrate the possibility of ethical relationality within schools.

Schools have the possibility to become inclusive sites for all learners, by embodying the (inter/intra)-connected nature of ecological sensibilities of education. The binaries perpetuated by positivist and absolutist theories may fade as the result of much broader understandings. This will not negate learning of content, rather it will require an increased level of richness, recursion, relation, and rigor (Doll, 1993) through learning as reflective processes. By necessity, the differences and redundancies possessed by students and teachers—as change agents within the complexities of collective interactions—will support the pedagogical dialogical ideal (Ellsworth, 1997).

Critical Possibilities

In this section, I challenge the mechanistic and positivistic educational modus operandi (Kincheloe, 2005c). Through a critical lens I suggest that positivism, as I have discussed previously, is no longer an adequate schema to consider learning and learners in the context of education. A critical focus on pedagogy affords for empowerment and emancipation: "fostering decisive agency that does not take apposition of neutrality in its contextual examination of the various forces that impact the human condition" (Kirylo, 2013, p. xxi). This challenge to historically adequate models for teaching is a challenge for classroom teachers and administrators because "the power of mechanistic psychology and positivist forms of education to label and categorize is so pervasive" (Steinberg & Kincheloe, 2018, p. 31). The potential "safety" associated with these top-down deficit models has allowed for the control structures of a perceived accountability where failures can be readily identified and fixed through positivistic controls.

According to Steinberg and Kincheloe (2018), critical educators are strongly concerned with the politics that are associated with teaching and learning. They agree with Freire (1996) in the fact that there is no education that is disconnected from the political. The information, knowledges, and understandings that are privileged to become curricular are determined through overseeing political structures. "Which knowledges are legitimated and which knowledges are erased always reflect who possesses power and who does not" (Steinberg & Kincheloe, 2018, p. 35). Steinberg and Kincheloe (2018) suggest that critical teachers actively support students in the "study of the world around them, learning who they are and what has shaped them in the process" (p. 31). It is this recognition by both students and teachers that we are in an ongoing state of becoming by constantly and dynamically acting on and being acted upon.

Learning and cognition are no longer considered by some scholars to be exclusively individual activities—learning occurs co-implicitly within the confluence of the individual and social (Davis et al., 2015; Steinberg & Kincheloe, 2018; Cozolino, 2012). In fact, Steinberg and Kincheloe (2018) suggest that there have been negative effects associated with individualistic understanding:

> As with learning itself, cognition is both an individual and a social action. Where its individual dimension ends and the social begins is not discernable; indeed, the individual and the social cannot be separated. This is what positivistic observers have missed in the process, causing great harm to children and adults. (pp. 30-31)

Through peer-to-peer dialogue, professional colleagues may be able to support each other in advancing paradigms towards a more open understanding of curriculum possibilities (Zhang, 2018). Henderson and Gornik (2007) stated: "When professionals advance a paradigm, they are making two interrelated moves. They are framing and justifying the organizing problem of their field, and they are stating how this problem should be studied, and they hope, resolved" (p. 10).

When we consider learning and cognition through this alternative framework of engaging with others it is possible to (re)consider how students' experiences are fundamental to learning. Building on John Dewey's (1938) understandings that higher levels of cognition and learning can occur when students' affective experiences are considered, teachers may be able to incorporate *generative themes* (Shor, 1992; Freire, 1996) into pedagogies. These "topics taken from students' lived experience that is compelling and controversial enough to elicit their excitement and commitment" (Steinberg & Kincheloe, 2018, p. 32) may provide opportunity to develop a love for learning and a sense of critical consciousness (Freire, 1996; Seidel & Jardine, 2014; Gruenewald, 2003).

Self-study

Self-study research exists in the confluence of one's biography and history (Bullough and Pinnegar, 2001; Bullough & Gitlin, 1995), whereby the researcher situates themselves inside the process (Samaras, 2010). Self-study requires the reflexive researcher to be: self-initiated and focused, improvement-aimed, interactive, multiple, primarily qualitative methods focused, exemplar-based in validation (LaBoskey, 2004, pp. 842-853). Self-study is personally situated and collaborative inquiry which improves learning, provides opportunity for knowledge generation, and is transparent. (Samaras, 2011).

Self-study is a recognition of the intersection of self and other. Self-study is positioned as autobiographical, cultural, and political (Hamilton & Pinnegar, 1998) which makes it inherently critical. Britzman (1986) shares that connecting our-self and our-history "allows the individual critical insight into both the nature of her/his relationship to individuals, institutions, cultural values, and political events, and the ways in which these social relationships contribute to the individuals' identity, values, and ideological perspectives" (p. 452). Self-study is not simply a focus on the self and deviates from autobiography and autoethnography because self-study engages with the evolving space between the self and the practice and the other and requires dialogues with critical friends.

Personal history self-study occurs through the engagement of the researchers with their life experiences beginning in the autobiographical and recursively, collaboratively, and reflexively making explicit the connections of practice to theory through critical dialogues. Personal history self-study may afford self-knowing and (re)forming a professional identity, modeling, and testing effective reflection, and pushing the boundaries of teaching (Samaras et al., 2004).

Considering the generative and dialogical

When comparing the goals of the teacher in a paradigm of control to those teaching in a more open paradigm, Doll (1993) claims that "in the former the teacher wishes to achieve precision in presentation; in the latter the teacher wishes 'to keep the dialogue going'" (p. 169). This is indicative of a critical shift towards a belief in the power of a generative process (Steinberg & Kincheloe, 2018). According to Gómez (2002), "the basis of the process of learning, implies not just talking or discussing issues but promoting cooperation, motivation, self-confidence, solidarity, and thus instrumental learning of any kind" (p. 13). No longer is the role of the teacher to distribute knowledge to passive students; instead, school becomes the place where educators can empower silenced students' voices and schooling becomes the ongoing process of reflective dialogical generative learning.

The responsibility of educators is no longer knowledge distribution and should be (re)imagined to consider learning as a reflective and identity-transforming process rather than a fixed end goal. Davies (2006) elaborates by advocating:

> Our responsibility [as educators] lies inside social relations and inside a responsibility to and for *oneself in relation to the other*—not oneself as a known entity, but oneself in process, unfolding or folding up, being done or undone, in relation to the other, again and again. (p. 436)

Educators can create the possibilities for ethical spaces (Ermine, 2007) that afford for an ongoing productive dialogical tension (Hasebe-Ludt et al., 2009; Donald, 2009). As a result, dialoguers may be able to see ideas and beliefs as non-dichotomous interactions, not succumbing to each other, but rather braided together (Donald, 2009).

This dialogical shift in education where pedagogies do not position students and educators within a competitive hierarchical structure may afford for students and educators to be positioned as co-learners, engaged in ongoing acts of critical thinking. Freire (1996) advises:

> True dialogue cannot exist unless the dialoguers engage in critical thinking—thinking which discerns an indivisible solidarity between the world and the people and admits of no dichotomy between them—thinking which perceives reality as process, as transformation, rather than a static entity. (p. 73)

Schön (1983) suggests that it is through dialogue with educational stakeholders and through public inquiry that we may challenge our own understandings, this will allow us to "reflect on [our] own tacit understandings" (pp. 296-297). By engaging in this generative dialogical process, we can bring to light our taken for granted assumptions and reflexively disrupt our own conceptions while fostering a transformative impact on the thoughts and understandings of others (Doll, 1993). Krammer and Mangiardi (2012) support the necessity for exchange of idea through dialogue when they state that "a solitary act of reflection can engender only limited understandings; but the dynamic interplay of two critically questioning minds can transform, create, and expand each participant's understandings" (p. 43). The educator's role is changed through (re)imagining a possibility of facilitating students through dialogue and interactions which support internal, reflective growth.

Steinberg and Kincheloe (2018) suggest that by inadequately considering learning through the lens of isolation, and in the "absence of relationship—Westerners have ignored difference" (p. 37). They go on to advocate that "critical teachers, aware of these Western failings, seek relationship and dialogue with those who see the world differently" (p. 37). In this context Doll (1993) posits "the teaching role, here, is ancillary not causative. This is not to lessen teaching's role but to change it" (p. 102). He goes on to posit:

> In this frame, where curriculum becomes process, learning and understanding come through dialogue and reflection. Learning and understanding are made (not transmitted) as we dialogue with others and reflect on what we and they have said—as we "negotiate passages" between ourselves and others, between texts and ourselves. (p. 156)

Students may become empowered to challenge or question what and how they are thinking about a concept. Through these attempted articulations, students may share what they are struggling with or feeling troubled by in a "space of possibilities that is opened up through the exploration of the current space of the possible" (Davis & Sumara, 2007, p. 58). As Ellsworth (1997) contends, "dialogue in education relies upon, namely 'understanding' and 'misunderstanding'" (p. 15), which allows for students to shape who they are relative to the process of learning.

Alternative pedagogies of hope and love

Hope is the unwavering ability to imagine that which is unknown. Hope allows us to envision alternative possibilities. Hope allows for the possibility to disrupt current entrenched understandings and beliefs and to recognize that there may be other ways to view, interpret, or name the world. Eloquently, Smith (1999) suggests that:

> the aim of interpretation, it could be said, is not just another interpretation but human freedom, which finds its light, identity and dignity in those few brief moments when one's lived burdens can be shown to have their source in too limited a view of things. (p. 29)

Markides (2017) claims, "in a Western worldview 'hope' becomes fragmented and measurable—*acceptable research*" (p. 293), research that is still bounded by a history of quantifiable commensurability. Perhaps the quest for commensurable grand narratives (Lyotard, 1984) may cause the exclusion or *explaining away* (Khun, 1996) of any data that is considered as an outlier as well as many things that are challenging to quantify. Creating a justification for assessing only that which can be measured. But schools can act as places of hope, where openness and dialogue may provide the recognition that we are all in a state of *becoming* as the result of the process of learning (Britzman, 2003). Schools can become places where humans may begin to understand that much of what is learned, understood, and embodied—those things which may turn out to matter the most—exist within the realm of the incommensurable.

Jardine et al. (2014) claim, "teachers and students alike are each *becoming someone* because of what they have learned and remembered" (p. 38). Renert (2011) suggests, "since school is a social institution situated at the intersection between present society and the promise of what society may become, educators are more likely to succeed in their work with messages of hope and possibility" (p. 25). Seidel (2014) advises us "to understand that the person we are becoming is also being shaped by these institutions might propel us into action, trying to change the institution's identity and character, to make it more humane and generous" (pp. 145-146). Goodson (1999) contends that schools can be a place to support the idea of *moral* witnessing—the belief that the world is in a constant state of construction with no definitive truth, only truths in given contexts. This understanding of constant change is parallel to that of flux (Little Bear, 2000; Kovach, 2017)—whereby knowledges need be enacted in ethical ways with a good heart. All of these scholars share similar hopefully concerned visions for what schools and schooling may become, given the opportunity, and, the appropriate leadership.

School can be the place for praxis to be fostered. It is the emancipatory classroom that "offers the space for change, invention, spontaneous shifts, that can serve as a catalyst" (hooks, 1994, p. 11)—a catalyst for hope, opportunity, and empowerment. Freire (1996) suggests that hope cannot exist without dialogue, "nor yet can dialogue exist without hope. Hope is rooted in men's incompletion, from which they move out in constant search—a search which can be carried out only in communication with others" (p. 72). Educators may be able to support the complexities of the classroom—individuals enmeshed as part of a collective—through pedagogies of hope and love. Clingan (2015) claims that "when we act from love the results transform for the good. With love our laws can change, our systems can change, and we can in fact begin to heal the world" (n.p.). Through the (re)consideration of the Albertan narrative of school and schooling, the human/more-than-human artificial dichotomy may be dis/de/un-popularized as the soul hegemonic myth and may be subsumed through transformative pedagogies of hope and love. bell hooks (2001, 2003) defines love as a combination of care, commitment, knowledge, responsibility, respect, and trust, where all these characteristics work together to help us serve each other. Love offers the possibility for growth and change—to support us in becoming who we are meant to be (Wagamese, 2011a, 2011b, 2016, 2019).

It is my hope that all educators may come to understand that the vision of the absolutist and reductionist teaching paradigms are no longer adequate to support students as they move into uncertain futures—futures that are not yet solidified. As Doll (1993) suggests education "is a process—not of transmitting what is known but exploring what is unknown" (p. 155). It is therefore the responsibility of an ethical education to be both dependent and accountable for the unknown (Britzman, 2011, 2013; Beckers & Hannula, 2013). Doll (1993) also states that, "a constructive curriculum is one that emerges through the actions and interactions of its participants" (p. 162). The divergent possibilities of the not-yet-imagined ecological sensibilities may allow for students to consider schools as places—no longer disconnected from life outside of school (Dewey, 1915)—where vivid memories of community, complexity, and collectivity facilitate long-term connections to the process of learning (Kimmerer, 2014). Through the embodiment of ethical relationality Donald (2016) posits that, "people face each other as relatives and build trusting relationships by connecting with others in respectful ways. In doing so, we demonstrate that we recognize one another as fellow human beings and work hard to put respect and love at the forefront of our interactions" (p. 10). By (re)imagining schools and schooling as place, educators and learners may embody the transformative pedagogy of love.

Possibilities for Instructional Leadership, Constrained in the LQS

The new Leadership Quality Standard (Alberta Education, 2017a), the new standard by which administrators' competency is evaluated relative to, in

Alberta and its related indicators have been constructed with language which is divergent from the previous iteration. The competencies indicate a tendency towards a recognition and openness towards the importance of relationality and social accountability Additionally, there seems to be an implicit revisioning of educational leadership to construct/nurture/foster/draw-out teacher realizations and awareness' to a multiplicity of epistemologies, metaphors, and pedagogies—the emergently possible. It appears that within the constraints of the LQS generative and critical learning experiences can be afforded whereby "supportive, dialogical and interactive social relations in critical learning situations can promote cooperation, democracy, and positive social values, as well as fulfill needs for communication, esteem and poeticized learning" (Kahn & Keller, 2008, p. 29).

Instructional leadership may be able to disrupt stagnant education and leadership pedagogies. Through ethical and engaged learning opportunities teachers may be able to enact a more inclusive, divergent, and hopeful curricula that considers the complexities associated with ecological sensibilities. Through this reconsideration we may understand "that the purpose of education is to enable students to become critical thinkers and good human beings, [by] rejecting the notion that the primary purpose of education is economic growth and immediate financial success for students" (Robertson, 2013, p. 22). Perhaps teachers may begin to recognize that "teaching like learning is not about convergence onto a pre-established truth, but about divergence—about broadening what can be known and done" (Davis & Sumara, 2007, p. 64). An (inter/intra)-connectivity whereby all aspects of schooling are better understood as intimately connected—enmeshed in the confluence of collective understandings. As Weber (2017) suggests, "this world is not populated by singular, autonomous, sovereign being. It comprises a constantly oscillating network of dynamic interactions in which one thing changes through the change of another" (p. 14). It is precisely these connections fostered by effective instructional educational leadership—incommensurable and co-evolutionary—that may challenge the commonplace positivist paradigms that have been normalized within schools.

An argument for redress of instructional leadership possibilities

Encouraging, supporting, and facilitating educators to embody alternative paradigms for knowing, teaching, and learning—paradigms which recognize the complexity of the entanglements between all entities—will allow students and educators to (re)story (Kovach, 2017) and (re)imagine their identities (Lyle, 2017). If we consider that schools are not places where we simply acquire the correct information to prepare for a known future, we may instead envision schools as places that may influence emergent identities where we learn to be humble and vulnerable members of an as-yet-unimagined society.

Supporting this shift in the role of education will require educators to exercise reflexivity and actively support reflexivity within their students. By knowing oneself in a non-Cartesian, wholistic sense—in relation to others as (inter/intra-)connected with the environment—educators and students might understand themselves and learning in more emergent ways.

As Coulthard (2014) suggests, "our senses of self are thus dependent on and shaped through our complex relations with others" (p. 28). This fluid and emergent sense of self comes as the result "of incorporating [the] reassembled past, seeming present, and anticipated future into an internalized dynamically changing story of self" (Kraehe, 2015; McAdams, 2001, 2013, as cited in Lyle, 2017, p. 3). Looking inward and seeing that we embody our histories, knowledges, and experiences will allow us to recognize that we are continually and mutually co-impacting each other.

Conclusion

The paradox of teaching in a knowledge society is while schools and teachers are expected to create the human skills and capacities that enable knowledge economies to survive and succeed, they are also expected to teach the compassion, sense of community, and emotional sympathy that mitigate and counteract the immense problems that knowledge economies create. (Hargreaves, 2003)

The top-down impacts of positivist and absolutist paradigms still permeate the knowledge economies of the Western Canadian world and its education systems. As a result, the demands on teachers to be accountable for their impacts on students' knowledge and understandings of taken-as-prescriptive curricular outcomes can supersede the social and emotional well-being of the whole child. Hard data from formal summative and formative assessments drive the ways in which teachers are expected to address problematic individual and collective knowledge deficits. Objective measurement indicators of learning that can be quantified and proven to be commensurable through scientific method are chosen as addressable and therefore important because there is an "unblinking assumption that science has cornered the market on truth" (Kimmerer, 2014, p. 160). What is potentially misunderstood is the social and affective conditions that cannot be universal and therefore unsettle the objectivist's paradigm. As Bourdieu (2017) elegantly suggests:

> the practical privilege in which all scientific activity arises never more subtly governs that activity (insofar as science presupposes not only an epistemological break but also a *social* separation) than when, unrecognised as privilege, it leads to an implicit theory of practice which is the corollary of neglect of the social conditions in which science is possible. (p. 1)

An unfortunate consequence of the impacts of a knowledge economy is the increased fragmentation of what society perceives as the teacher's role relative to what teachers perceive as their role. Additionally, in this context Davies (2006) suggests, "students work very hard to embody themselves as appropriate and appropriated subjects" (p. 433)—automatons without agency. Accountability to commensurable indicators of student success is now part of the profession's responsibility, but so too are the incommensurable measures. So how can educators ethically and consciously negotiate the spaces of professional learning given the pressures to meet the needs of students and stakeholder perceptions of what education should be?

As systems, we have begun to address the social and emotional well-being of students in addition to their academics while being ill-prepared to do so. While supporting the social and emotional needs of students have always been understood as important by many effective and caring educators and scholars, these needs are only now becoming part of district and provincial mandates. In a dynamic, social, helping profession such as teaching—envisioned through the objective and rational lenses—not being able to fix systemic problems, such as social and emotional traumas, or the ineffectiveness of taking up curricula in prescriptive manner, has a negative impact on educators. Solutions associated with these issues can no longer be, in good conscience, reduced to positivistic cause-effect relations, nor can students be assumed to be homogenous groups of mutually exclusive individuals. Therefore, the safety and essential distancing by educators to afford for objectivity of a curricula is no longer adequate. What students need and deserve is a curriculum that affords for pedagogies of love.

Note

1 The Tyler Model of education consists of creating objectives, determining content, selecting methods, and evaluating understandings. While it is possible for this model to be interpreted through multiple paradigms, current enactments are inextricably aligned with those of objectivist and positivistic scientific methodological convergent pedagogies.

· 3 ·

ENACTING SELF-STUDY

The purpose of this research is to illuminate alternative possibilities for education in Alberta. Through a personal history self-study I continue to disrupt my current rationalist, reductionist pedagogies and paradigms that are perpetuated by top-down expectations and associated popular literatures. Schools, administrators, and educators are at a rapidly changing moment in Alberta given the incorporation of legislative/evaluative expectations of the new TQS (Alberta Education, 2017c), LQS (Alberta Education, 2017a), and the possible implementation of a new regressive curriculum. Additionally, expectations for the incorporation of the Foundational Principles of High School Redesign (see Alberta Education, 2018a) call on high school teachers and administrators to challenge preconceived notions of what schooling in the context of high school can or should become.

Sharing stories regarding my perceived understandings and possible impacts on teaching practices, paradigms, and pedagogies is a critical act because as Cruikshank (2000) shares, "storytelling can construct meaningful bridges in disruptive situations. When potential for division emerges, successful resolution often involves demonstrating how a story can reframe issues by providing larger context" (p. 4). The larger context of this study is a hopeful disruption that may support paradigmatic evolution within Alberta of teacher's singular, reductionistic epistemological and ontological understanding of school towards that of an evolution. An evolution that sees the divergence of possibilities for education and pedagogies as potential indication of an increased robustness through diversification and entanglement of prominent metaphors of education rather than the perpetuation of singular pedagogical and didactical correctness.

The more focused context of this study is an inward iterative reflexive consideration of who I am as an educator, how my lived affective history has brought me to this moment, and how I have worked to find coherence in seemingly incoherent paradigms. By sharing autobiographical narratives with critical friends and engaging in generative dialogical encounters I have developed a more wholistic understanding of my own educational experiences.

The primary research question in this study was, "How can I use self-study to better understand Albertan education in this current moment, and how and in what ways can my current pedagogical understandings allow for divergent future educational possibilities?" Several sub questions were considered and expanded upon through the self-study process. The questions are as follows:

- What were my first educational memories?
- How and in what ways did teachers positively or negatively impact my educational experiences? Has my understanding of these impacts changed over time?
- What were my early beliefs regarding the purpose of education and what metaphors are related to those beliefs?
- What were my beliefs regarding education upon entering preservice teacher training? What were they afterward?
- When did I first begin to understand that education was politically motivated?
- Are there any specifically impactful events that occurred within my educational experiences? How did these events impact understandings of education?
- Who have been my life influences that have crossed into educational experiences?

Through autobiographical writing, sharing my narratives with critical friends, and then reformulating thoughts through public witnessing of my stories have served to evoke a deeper understanding of my affective experiences while revealing some of the events/moments/activities that served to perturbate my paradigmatic lens and understandings of education. Better understanding the evolution of my own practice as I have negotiated the complexities of enacting the local *enabling constraints* (Davis et al., 2015) of Foundational Principles of High School Redesign and the TQS and LQS, I have come to better understand the multiple contextual and relational experiences associated with the complexities of education and educational leadership work.

In this chapter I describe and share examples of the study's research methodology, my epistemological and ontological foundations, and theoretical framework. Effectively, this chapter serves to continue my shared personal narrative regarding the trustworthiness of the study and my ethical consideration as I proceed throughout the process of carrying out the study. Furthermore, discussions around epistemological and ontological considerations will be embedded.

Carspecken (2013) suggests that epistemology refers to the suppositions that we make about knowledge and how it can be acquired. According to Wilson (2008) epistemology refers to:

> the study of the nature of thinking and knowing. It involves the theory of how we come to have knowledge, or how we know that we know something.... Epistemology is tied in to ontology, in that what I believe to be "real" is going to impact on the way that I think about that "reality." (p. 33)

My epistemological position is rooted in social constructivism which is why I am so drawn to a shift towards ecological understandings and complexity; however, definitions can never be that simple. I know that the language that we use and how it is interpreted can evoke contradictory understandings. Sumara et al. (2001) provide an excellent example of how language and too restrictive of an understanding can cause contradictions when they state, "if all knowledge is understood to be socially constructed, then it makes no sense to suggest that hearts know how to beat, beavers know how to build dams, ecosystems know how to recover from unexpected perturbations, and so on" (p. 150). For this reason, I understand that knowledge is a constantly evolving, complex, social, and cultural construct—always in a state of flux (Little Bear, 2000; Kovach, 2017). I understand that knowledge is indistinguishable from the way that the knowledge was constructed—knowledge should be understood as relational. According to Davis et al. (2008), "knowing is not a matter of inert bits of information, but is inseparable from doing and being. Knowing is the dynamic of existence" (p. 225). Knowing is a reflective, recursive, evolution towards an embodied understanding—constantly revisited, revised, and re-evaluated. It is lived.

Metaphors are the means to help construct meaning within the realm of abstract ideas. When meaning is coherent within a subsumable schema it may be considered knowledge, but not in a static manner. Morrison (2008) suggests that knowledge is the result of a transformation of understandings whereby "knowledge is perpetually being constructed and reconstructed through the assimilation and accommodation of new knowledge to existing knowledge, thereby changing both the existing and new knowledge, rather than either being fixed and finite" (p. 25). These beliefs regarding epistemological grounding, as previously stated, are intimately connected to my ontological understandings.

Wilson (2008) describes ontology as "the theory and nature of existence, or the nature of reality.... [P]eople develop an ontological set of beliefs and take it on faith from there" (p. 33). What the "purpose" or reality of living is and the nature of being in the world I understand to be an evolving and highly contextual idea. However, I see the world as much more interconnected and chaotic than current hegemonic reductionistic paradigms would have one believe. I do not believe that the world is a matter of Newtonian or Cartesian simplicity, out there to be discovered.

I hope that it will become evident in the next section of this chapter that I hesitate to claim a specific or static epistemological or ontological stance. In a world that exists in a state of flux, my enmeshed epistemological and ontological understandings in any one moment could be inadequate in any other moment. This is not to say that I am perpetuating a state of "epistemological relativism" (McLaren, 2001, p. 701), in fact I claim that through an ongoing reflexivity I gain a deeper understanding of my epistemological and ontological frame. It is for these reasons that I outline my paradigmatic considerations in terms of complex and dynamic descriptors, and it is also why I enact methodology as a bricoleur.

Methodology

Methodology refers to the theory by which knowledge is obtained (Wilson, 2008), how research progresses given appropriate ethical and contextual considerations (Bloomberg & Volpe, 2016), or the justification as to why we intentionally select specific methods (Madden, 2013). In this research study, I am the only administrator participant supported by my critical friends which allows for the opportunity to gain a more in-depth understanding of my tenuous social and cultural context and how I may be perturbating teacher professional knowledges and paradigms (Creswell & Creswell, 2017).

From an epistemological and ontological perspective, knowledges, understandings, and realities in each building/school/division/region should be understood to emerge locally (collectively) while in constant tension with external expectations and policies. This research study is grounded in understanding the limitations of researcher objectivity. In fact, I find myself struggling within the intersubjective confluence as a witness to multiple social worlds and as the producer of my narrative representation (Kincheloe, 2005b). This is precisely why, in this research study, I will take on the role of bricoleur. As Kincheloe (2005c) suggests:

> What bricoleurs are exploring in this philosophical mode of inquiry are the nature and effects of the social construction of knowledge, understanding, and human subjectivity. Realizing the dramatic limitations of so-called objectivist assumptions about the knowledge production process, bricoleurs struggle to specify the ways perspectives are shaped by social, cultural, political, ideological, discursive, and disciplinary forces. Understanding the specifics of this construction process helps multiperspectival researchers choose and develop the methodological, theoretical, and interpretive tools they need to address the depictions of the world that emerge from it. (p. 337)

The following discussion of methodology continues a dialogue of the critical consciousness of how I worked to partition my own subjectivity as to the intersection of what I, as a researcher, currently know and that which is profound and yet-unknown (Kincheloe, 2005b).

Bricolage

The bricolage is rooted historically in the work of Lévi-Strauss (1966) *The Savage Mind* where he describes the possibility of the researchers-as-*bricoleur* as the handyman or handywoman. In this context the researcher-as-bricoleur actively constructs research methods from the disciplinary tools at hand rather than applying the universally accepted methodologies (Kincheloe et al., 2017). The bricolage is a recognition of the complexity of social interactions and associated research as well as the evolutionary nature of relationality. According to Kincheloe (2001):

> As researchers draw together divergent forms of research, they gain the unique insight of multiple perspectives. Thus, a complex understanding of research and knowledge production prepares bricoleurs to address the complexities of the social, cultural, psychological, and educational domains. Sensitive to complexity, bricoleurs use multiple methods to uncover new insights, expand and modify old principles, and re-examine accepted interpretations in unanticipated contexts. (p. 687)

This ecological sensibility calls on the bricoleur to allow for flexible, dynamic, and creative diversification of methodological relevance (Steinberg, 2012a; Kincheloe, 2001, 2005c).

The multimethodological nature of the bricolage allow the researcher-as-bricoleur the opportunity to widen their senses to a divergence of possibilities in inquiry, avoiding the reductionistic tendencies of singular research perspectives (Kellner, 1995). Researchers employing the bricolage are not necessarily tied to the axiomatic foundations of singular research methods.

> As bricoleurs recognize the limitations of a single method, the discursive structures of one disciplinary approach, what is missed by traditional practices of validation, the historicity of certified modes of knowledge production, the inseparability of knower and known, and the complexity and heterogeneity of all human experience, they understand the necessity of new forms of rigor in the research process. (Kincheloe, 2001, p. 681)

For this reason, social research is not, and should not be considered objective. It is therefore up to the researcher-as-bricoleur to recognize and embrace uncertainty and messiness within social contexts in the pursuit of robust research. According to Kincheloe et al. (2017), "the bricolage highlights the relationship between the researcher's ways of seeing and the social location of his or her personal history" (p. 244). By recognizing their active participation within and onto research, the bricoleur acknowledges their undeniable impact on social research through relationships which allows for their increased expertise in the relationality of power and oppression interior to disciplines (Steinberg & Kincheloe, 2018; Kincheloe, 2001, 2005b; Pinar, 2001; McLaren, 2001).

This dialogical and relational qualitative research study necessitates an interdisciplinary and responsive methodology that affords for the honoring and witnessing of an administrator's stories. As a result, there is no one method that can adequately accommodate for both the researcher as (emic) insider and (etic) outsider (Innes, 2009; Madden, 2013), while allowing for the recognition of "the unfolding context of the research situation" (Steinberg,

2012a, p. 184). Accordingly, the bricolage affords for what many of us already understand: that "we occupy a scholarly world with faded disciplinary boundary lines. Thus, the point need not be that bricolage should take place—it already has and is continuing" (Kincheloe, 2001, p. 863).

The bricolage is a process that serves as an acknowledgment of the complexity that has been ignored within social research (Kincheloe, 2001). The bricoleur works to uncover the interrelated nature of social research "focusing on the webs of relationships instead of simply things-in-themselves" (Kincheloe, 2005c, p. 323). The complex interactions and relationality of this type of research necessitates the reconsideration of a methodological framework in an active manner rather than a passive and static methodological stance.

Personal history self-study

> *To know the past is to know oneself as an individual and as a representative of a socio-historical moment in time; like others each person is a victim, vehicle, and ultimately a resolution of a culture's dilemmas. (Bullough & Gitlin, 1995, p. 25)*

Self-study research exists in the confluence of biography and history (Bullough and Pinnegar, 2001), whereby the researcher situates themselve inside the process (Samaras, 2010). Self-study is a recognition of a turn in educational research that acknowledges the intersection of self and other. Self-study is "autobiographical, historical, cultural, and political and takes a thoughtful look at texts read, experiences had, people known and ideas considered" (Hamilton & Pinnegar, 1998, p. 236). This place of complex, contextual, and irreproducible interactions is at the center of self-study research. Britzman (1986) shares that connecting our-self and our-history:

> Allows the individual critical insight into both the nature of her/his relationship to individuals, institutions, cultural values, and political events, and the ways in which these social relationships contribute to the individuals' identity, values, and ideological perspectives. In this way, individuals do have the capacity to participate in shaping and responding to the social forces which directly affect their lives. (p. 452)

The everchanging and evolving space for personal research necessitates us not to focus specifically on the self but rather on the space between the self and the practice and the other.

According to LaBoskey (2004) the characteristics required for self-study methodology necessitate self-studies are:

- Self-initiated and focused
- Improvement-aimed
- Interactive
- Multiple, primarily qualitative methods
- Exemplar-based validation (pp. 842-853)

In a similar vein, Samaras (2011) suggests a five foci framework for self-study research which is summarized in Table 4.

Table 4. Five Foci Framework for Self-study, Adapted from Samaras (2011, pp. 72-73)

	Focus	Methodological Component
1	Personal situated inquiry	Self-study is self-initiated and draws on the practitioner's experience
2	Critical collaborative inquiry	Self-study extends beyond one's personal views, exposing biases, and extends individual's understandings through the utilization of critical friends' dialogue and discourse
3	Improved learning	Through disruptive challenging of the known, the "so what" of practices are broadened. The learning of the self and the field is improved
4	Transparent and systematic research process	The iterative dialogical process of questioning and critique affords for possibilities to reframe, re-evaluate, and revisit understanding from both insider and outsider perspectives (Innes, 2009)
5	Knowledge generation and presentation	Self-study challenges what is understood as knowledge and broadens what is accepted as knowledge generation. Self-study necessitates the publicization of new knowledges and understandings

In a similar manner as Samaras et al. (2004) I understand personal history as:

> those formative, contextualized experiences that have influenced teachers' thinking about teaching and their own practice. Personal history research is reviewed as the historical or life experiences related to personal and professional meaning making for teachers and researchers. This includes both the autobiographical and life-history research of teacher educators' personal history work about themselves as well as teacher educators' work in using a personal history approach with their teacher-students towards improving teaching practice at both K-12 and university levels. (pp. 909-910)

Personal history self-study is a variation of self-study research that helps the researcher to engage with their lived-history and influences as another means to inform their reflexive process. Personal history self-study has allowed me as the researcher and the primary participant to help unpack and reconstruct my affective history in order to inform my professional and personal identity formation. This has in turn brought deeper meaning to my pedagogical understandings and made explicit the connections of my practice to theory (Samaras et al., 2004). I understand teaching to be an *autobiographical act* (Pinar & Grummet, 1976) that impacts the ways in which we understand knowing, learning, and teaching. Foundational to this personal history self-study research process were the following three possibilities for teaching as defined by Samaras et al. (2004)

1) self-knowing and forming—and reforming—a professional identity;
2) modeling and testing effective reflection; and,
3) pushing the boundaries of teaching. (p. 913)

These three possibilities for personal history self-study formed the framework for the organization of reporting out data that was collected as part research which can be found in subsequent chapters. For the remainder of this section, I will elaborate on each of these organizational possibilities.

Self-knowing and forming a professional identity is intimately connected to reflexivity and autobiography. Through self-study and growing in capacity for self-knowing I have grown in the understanding of the why I do what I do. By unpacking and revisiting the enmeshed and affective past I have allowed myself to envision a broader possible future. In a similar manner Bullough and Gitlin (1995) share;

> The writing of autobiographies does not free teachers from their histories but rather enables them to take charge of those histories, to assert ownership, and to recognize their place as actors who can shape contexts and as authors who have before them choices that matter. (p. 25)

Reflective acts become those of reflexivity when we "consider what is not obvious and what is yet to become because a grounding in personal experiences encourages consciousness and being awake to themselves and to the contexts in which they are embedded" (Samaras et al., 2004, p. 915).

Modeling and testing effective reflection seem to be a key to challenging and reimagining the possibilities for education. While there is a great deal of emphasis on self-reflection in preservice teacher training, time and the complexity of teaching life can become barriers to growth opportunities of self-study for practicing teachers and administrators. Through personal history self-study and its autobiographical provocation, we can disrupt the perception of the objectivity of teaching, learning, and knowing and provide opportunities to better know who we are as teachers.

Pushing the boundaries of teaching may come from a better understanding of self through personal history self-study. Samaras et al. (2004) suggest that personal history self-study may allow teachers to "examine the inconsistencies involved in their teaching and showcase their failings so that they and others, especially their students, might learn from their mistakes" (p. 924). Additionally, personal history self-study can provide opportunities for teachers to transform their personal pedagogies. Reflection on personal histories may help teachers to better understand the multiplicity of affective histories and associated understandings that students bring with them into learning spaces.

I took on personal history self-study through a critical and complexity-focused ecological lens—working to challenge and disrupt my own sacrosanct understandings while broadening possibilities by considering complex connectivities. The recursive and iterative process that I undertook involved autobiographical writing, interpreting critical friend feedback, and rewriting/reporting. Throughout these processes I was challenged to (re)consider what I understood about how I came to this moment and professional identity.

Autobiography

Self-study as well as teaching are autobiographical acts (Samaras, 2011; Samaras et al., 2004; Bullough & Pinnegar, 2001). Bullough and Pinnegar (2001) share their 14 guidelines to quality autobiography wherein they claim, "self-study points to a simple truth, that to study a practice is simultaneously to study self: a study of self-in-relation to other" (p. 14). Overall, as I read and reread the 14 guidelines it became increasingly apparent that autobiographical research is an ethical act of interconnected storytelling—sharing truths about struggles, interpreted realties, genuine learning opportunities, and possibilities for divergent reimagining.

Autobiography can serve as an opportunity for growth, reflection, and reinterpretation. Autobiographical writing required me to look back and unpack what was once taken for granted. Autobiography has "traumatically" exposed me to my own failings and short comings of the past through the interpretive lens of today. Autobiography required me to grapple with my own identity and the identities others impose on me. "It is that struggle and its resolve to develop ourselves in ways that transcend the identities that others have constructed for us that bonds the projects of autobiography and education" (Grumet, 1990, p. 324).

Grumet (1990) shares the following thoughts regarding the looking back at towards our lived experiences whereby:

> any writing and reading of our lives presents us with the challenge that is at the heart of every educational experience: making sense of our lives in the world. Autobiography becomes a medium for both teaching and research because each entry expresses the particular peace its author has made between the individuality of his or her subjectivity and the intersubjective and public character of meaning. The wound that haunts our consciousness by severing our private lives from our public world may begin to repair itself, at least on the level of text, as the languages of both worlds and their ways of being mingle in educational theory and practice. There is no formula for this relation. It is tuned to every writer and reader and to the situation they share. (p. 324)

Ultimately, autobiography in self-study can serve as the medium for reflexivity—a catalyst for reimagination. In this personal history self-study, autobiographical writing served as data that began dialogical moments with critical friends that afforded for drawing out themes, uncovering problems, and perturbating growth.

Narrative and story

The truth about stories is that's all we are. (King, 2003, p. 2)

Hinchman and Hinchman (1997) suggest that narratives are contextual, experiential, and sense-making by nature. They share the following definition: "Narratives (stories) in the human sciences should be defined provisionally as discourses with a clear sequential order that connect events in a meaningful way for a definite audience and thus insights about the world and/or people's experiences of it" (p. xvi). Goodson and Gill (2011) posit that the terms narratives and stories can be considered interchangeably because they share the following common features:

- temporality—all narratives encompass a sequence of events;
- meaning—personal significance and meaning are externalized through the telling of lived experiences;

- social encounter—all narratives are told to an audience and will inevitably be shaped by the relationship between the teller and the listener. (p. 4)

As mentioned in previous sections of this chapter, these characteristics of narrative/story are similar to those of personal history self-study. In fact, the externalizational necessity of self-study draws on story in an autobiographical sense as part of an identity formation process because "identity and narrative are intrinsically connected" (Goodson & Gill, 2011, p. 6). Lyons and LaBoskey (2002) suggest that all narratives:

- capture intentional human actions through developing knowledge;
- express the inner thinking of the characters in a socially and contextually nuanced situation;
- show interconnections to others within the stories;
- associate others identities as a consequence of the story;
- take different perspectives while concentrating on interpretation.

Clandinin and Connelly (1990) challenge more traditional fields of inquiry by proposing the possibilities that could be afforded through reconsidering teaching and curriculum through narratives. They suggest that, "the narrative study of experience brings body to mind and mind to body; it connects autobiography to action and an intentional future; it connects these to social history and direction" (p. 245). For Grumet (1990):

> Narratives of educational experience challenge their readers and writers to find both individuality and society, being and history and possibility in their texts. It is a brave company of educators who forsake simplistic polarities of individual and society to write, to read and to do scholarly work in these ways. It challenges feminists to encode the body and the idioms of meaningful lived relations without abandoning the disciplines of knowledge. It challenges teachers to listen to stories and to hear their resonance in the distant orchestration of academic knowledge. And it invites all of us, no matter how wide our disillusion, to notice how existence quickens us with joy surpassing despair. (p. 323)

All truths are stories. Collective stories interpreted through time and memory. Cruikshank (2000) suggests that storytelling can establish connections "between past and future, between people and place, among people whose opinions diverge" (p. 2). Stories serve to acknowledge our experiences, our feelings, and our insights. Stories allow us to share who we are—who we are as individuals and as part of a collective community. Margaret Kovach (2017) states, it is by hearing stories we can re-story these experiences "through our own lens, gaze, and perspective" (p. 227). This re-storying helps us make sense of a world larger than our own. "By allowing for the articulation of personal experience and shared values, stories connect families, tribes, and nations, generate culture, and link us to a group mind" (Cozolino, 2012, p. 188).

Stories give voice to those who have lost theirs. Stories help to foster empathy. Stories help to heal and build community (Kovach, 2017). Stories can challenge what is known to be true and shine a light on areas where we can grow. "It is through stories that customs and values are taught and shared" (Little Bear, 2000, p. 80). Stories can support in the development of wisdom. Our stories empower us. Stories take time; they require an attention to detail—nuances that necessitate an understanding of culture and epistemology. Unfortunately, the commodity of time is not one that we are always willing to spare or spend.

As part of my role as an administrator, I find that much of my time with parents or teachers is spent listening. Sitting quietly until they have had the chance to make their point or tell their story—creating and making meaning. It is a trusting interaction between the storyteller and the listener-as-interpreter that makes storytelling so important. As Cruikshank (2000) shares:

> Meaning does not inhere in events but involves weaving those events into stories that are meaningful at the time. Events, after all, are stories known directly only to those who experience them and interpret them to others, who in turn make their own interpretations of what they hear. (p. 2)

I am occasionally the buffer between an irate parent who needs me to be witness to their frustration and the teacher or student on the other side of the story. This is part of my work—my work to build trust. From my experience, parents want to be heard, parents want to know that you care for their children, but most of all they want to be able to trust me. As we are all aware, trust takes a great deal of time to build with adults and with youth who have had their sense of trust broken before and can instantaneously be broken again. I am convinced now more than ever that this trust comes from taking the time to witness, to hear, and to share stories.

By recognizing that our paradigms and those of others may be incommensurable, we can then begin to consider different vantage points. The idea of flux or fluidity (Kovach, 2017) when interpreted through the metaphor of a surfer riding a wave that Rupert Ross (1996) uses as part of his conversation with Moonhawk Alford, I find to be incredibly helpful. For, like the surfer, we are not riding on the present, but moving to where the waves will be—different than they were but similar—we move forward with our relationship trusting in our relationality. It is this comfort in relationality through the witnessing of stories that will allow us "not to extrapolate but rather to seek situational understanding" (Kovach, 2017, p. 221).

One of the many challenges that exist when witnessing stories in a participatory manner is the recognition of constant change. It is this constant change that can create an unsolvable paradox (Tuck, 2009) one which allows for the bricoleur to adjust and reconsider their understandings. Tuck (2009) suggests that "when met with an unsolvable paradox, all we can do with it is walk to a new vantage point" (p. 55). By recognizing the complexity of relationality and relationships, with their infinitude of strange attractors, variables, and influences we consider what it is truly like to work with other humans. It is this recognition of the tenuous state of the dynamic disequilibrium that we exist in that may challenge our own storied, experiential perception of reality. It is through my gathering/(re)collecting/writing of stories that I was able to better understand my life journey as well as the subtle perturbations that brought me to my current moment. Through the self-study of these stories, I was able to "make explicit the social processes one takes for granted as a culture member" (Steinberg, 2012a, p. 185).

In the next sections of this chapter, I share insights as to the logistics of the research study. I elaborate upon the specifics of who will be involved, and the context of location and data collection methods utilized.

Research Setting

This research study was timely as The Alberta Government instituted the new Teaching Quality Standard (TQS) (Alberta Education, 2017c) and the new Leadership Quality Standard (LQS) (Alberta Education, 2017a) beginning in September of 2019, looking to implement a new regressive curriculum. Additionally, the Foundational Principles for High School Redesign (Alberta Education, 2018b) are seeing a signification refocus and resurgence given its interconnection with the applications of the TQS and LQS at the primary and secondary school levels.

There is always flux in the political influences and ideologies in the province which in-turn impact education, sometimes subtly and other times violently. The transformation of education and curriculum are perturbated from the tensions between stakeholders: parents, students, community members, private industry, post-secondary institutions, etc. Meanwhile the memories of education's histories, embodied through the familiar profession serve to dampen fluctuations (Britzman, 2003; Ellsworth, 1997). Alberta is no exception. A province and its citizens which is world renowned for its education system ("PISA Worldwide Rankings", 2018), will always push-back against change.

I understand much of my work as a school administrator is to afford for disruptive dialogical opportunities to change education and perturbate teaching paradigms. I see myself as a risk-taker who envisions possibilities for more equitable, more empowering, and more inclusive education built on relationships with community. As Robinson (2011) suggest "leadership is not about building trust so that the hard work of improvement can happen later. It is about tackling the work in ways that build trust through learning and making progress together" (p. 43). This study has explored and interrogated my personal insights of change, change agents, and personal and collective perceptions of impact in the context of education.

Data Collection Methods

At the beginning of this chapter, I shared an extensive overview of my methodological understandings and considerations as they are relevant to the study. According to Madden (2012) "methodology is a justification of the use of a particular set of methods. Methods are what tools you use; a methodology is an explanation of why you use these tools" (p. 25). It is therefore in this frame that I briefly share the tools that will be employed.

Autobiographical writing was used as a starting point for dialogue with critical friends. Through recursively and iteratively reconsidering autobiographical writing, interpreting critical friend feedback, and rewriting/reporting, themes were drawn out. Through the iterative data collection process more autobiographical moments were drawn out; as a result, the reporting and data collection processes were woven together. There were numerous times that recollection of past pedagogies emerged as troubling and painful. However, as Clandinin (1995) suggests these moments are necessary to disrupt current practices.

> Without imagining, living, and telling new competing stories that question the plot line of the sacred story, little in my lived story as a teacher educator and little in the professional knowledge landscape can change. Without opening up to the many possible visions that serve as possible storylines, I may find myself no longer still learning to teach. (p. 31)

Through iterative, critical, dialogical, disruptive, autobiographical moments this personal history self-study took shape.

Trustworthiness

Within the context of this critical research self-study, trust and trustworthiness are intimately connected to who I am and how I am perceived. As Kovach (2017) states, "it is not simply about trust in the findings and "validation of the data"; it is about trust in the relationship" (p. 224). I believe that being transparent about how data was collected and why I choose to deal with data the ways that I did, add to the trustworthiness of this study (Madden, 2012). Therefore, I recognize and acknowledge that I enjoy the privilege of working as a school administrator which will not only bring me creditability with readers who happen to have administrative experiences. Additionally, I understand that there may be a possibility of a bimodal appreciation for administrators or educators who choose to read my research because of their similar or contradictory experiences or paradigms.

Richard Wagamese (2011) suggests that trust can be defined in the following manner:

> Trust is the spiritual by-product of innocence…. Innocence is more than lack of knowledge and experience, it's learning to look at the world with wonder. When we do that, we live in a learning way. Trust is the ability to open yourself to teachings, is the gateway for each of us to becoming who we were created to be…. Trust is, in fact, our first act of faith and our first step towards the principle of courage that will guide us. (p. 57)

The perception of trustworthiness is not simply a matter of whether the reader has faith in the data that I present. It cannot be that simple. Trustworthiness has to do with how readers will come to trust me as well. The trustworthiness of the stories that I share begins with the way by which I choose to articulate them, and then conclude by the ways in which readers choose and continue to choose to connect their histories to these stories to make coherence in their understanding. The validity of these stories becomes less about objectivity and more about relationality. It is therefore up to the reader to make sense, accept, deny, or struggle with the findings. As Mishler (1990) suggests, "focusing on trustworthiness rather than truth, displaces validation from its traditional location in a presumably objective neutral reality, and moves it to the social world—a world constructed in and through our discourse and actions, through praxis" (p. 420).

As mentioned previously, I understand trustworthiness of data and research finding to be more about a trust in who I am as researcher, my history as a community member, and the biases that I bring to the research through my previous experiences. I understand that trust emerges through relationality, and relationality is nurtured through knowing me—a relational trust. Relational trust in research or leadership is grounded in praxis. The trustworthiness of this research study, I claim, is founded on relationality (Kovach, 2017; Wilson, 2008). Following the framework of Robinson (2011) as adapted from Bryk and Schneider (2002) there are four key components to building relational trust, see Table 5.

Table 5. Determinants of Relational Trust and Indicators as Adapted from Robinson (2011)

Determinant of Relational Trust	Indicators
Interpersonally respectful	• Valuing the ideas of other • Listening carefully • Being open to influence
Personal regard for others	• Caring about others • Inviting reciprocal regard • Personal expressions of support
Competent in role	• Actively engaging in tough dialogue • Continued promotion of collective effort • Growth-minded promotion of expectation
Personal integrity	• Even tempered and consistent • Follow through consistently on commitments • Follow through on collective vision • Reaffirmation of primary principles (Bryk & Schneider, 2002)

I hope to embody these indicators in a good way throughout the three phases of this research: autobiographical writing, interpreting critical friend feedback, and rewriting/reporting. I was sure to consider these indicators as I reconsidered my own autobiographical recollections through the lenses of critical friends, recognizing that there is not always a coherent means to map another's understandings one-to-one onto my own understanding (Todd, 2003; Cruikshank, 2000). I believe using Robinson's (2011) determinants of relational trust was an important additional means to ground my observational and reflexive lens.

Validity

Personal history self-study requires a bricolage of methodological considerations and is subjective in nature. To increase the validity of this self-study research I was careful to incorporate the suggestions as laid out by Feldman (2003), see Table 6.

Table 6. Suggestions to Increase Validity in Self-Study as Adapted from Feldman (2003, pp. 27-28)

	Suggestion
1	more explicit description and identification of how data was collected;
2	a discussion of how the researcher constructed the representation of data;
3	an exploration of multiple ways of representing the same self-study;
4	evidence of the value of the changes that were promoted through the self-study

Ethical Considerations

"What is the proper balance between the interests of science and the thoughtful, humane treatment of people, who innocently, provide the data?" (Cohen, Manion, & Morrison, 2011a, pp. 66-67)

Throughout this research study, I took a similar stance to Steinberg (2012b) whereby I understand research to be a social theoretical act. It is important to once again acknowledge that I was the primary research participant, the nature of personal history self-study and the ethical consideration were those associated with recollections and considerations of critical feedback.

My research is contextually grounded and connected to culture and place. I feel that by recognizing that all my experiences were those of an individual nested within a collective influenced and impacted by infinitely many influences has served to eliminate thoughtlessness. I understand that I have recalled my life experiences in a non-linear manner. For, as Ezra Pound (1970) suggests:

> We do not know the past in chronological sequence. It may be convenient to lay it out anesthetized on the table with the dates pasted on here and there, but what we know we know by ripples and spirals eddying out from us and from our own time. (p. 60)

I know my past through what I understand now—A dynamic paradigm in flux creating a lens that allows for reimagination.

As Cohen et al. (2011a) suggest, "there are few absolutes [in research] and in consequence ethical principles may be open to a wide range of interpretation" (p. 71). And while the ethical code may help to state the responsibility of researchers in context of the research project, it is the interpretation, enactment, and embodiment of this code by the researchers that will support in building trust with the community. The pursuit of truth and trust should not proceed contrary to each other (Cohen et al., 2011b), ethically they should run parallel.

As mentioned previously, I was the primary participant in the study. I did engage in dialogue with several critical friends to help me externalize and critique my personal recollections. The critical friends that assisted my personal history self-study know me to varying extents and we share varying power dynamics; however, the power dynamics did not come into play due to the open, organic, critical, and dialogical nature of conversations.

Summary

Throughout this chapter I outlined the research design which included methodology, context, research setting, sample, and ethical consideration. Within this chapter's narrative I implicitly discussed how the methodology will afford for trustworthiness through relationality with critical friends. It should be understood that I see my work's trustworthiness as intimately connected to relationality and a trust of me as the researcher and author. In the next chapter I share some of the relevant autobiographical data that I used to ground this study and emergent themes categorized by the three possibilities for teaching as established by Samaras et al. (2004)

· 4 ·
A CRITICAL PERSONAL HISTORY SELF-STUDY

During this work, I have shared some of my personal history and positioning. I am a white, middle-class, privileged, male. I hold a position of power as a principal and school leader. Statistically, I am well educated. Through much of my work and writing I look for ways to decenter my power. At this point it is imperative that I preface this second to last chapter with some more information about how I've come to understand teaching.

As a student, I found a personal strength in the math and physical sciences, but writing was always a challenge for me. In fact, I despised writing most of the time. In my high school career, my lacking ability in writing was confirmed by grades. Perhaps it was because of the didactical focus on formulaic writing (five paragraph essay, with keyhole entries, themes, thesis, body, and conclusion), that once achieved never seemed to be adequate. Even now I find writing to be incredibly challenging. I think part of the struggle is that I look for beauty in the work that I do and I never seem to achieve that with writing. Writing has, for me anyway, been something where beauty is incommensurable, like love, something that just is and does not need to be measured or quantified. When I read the works of others, I am often inspired by the talents and insights that these authors possess and can express on paper. I am amazed how a few words can illicit such powerful emotions that reignite past experiences or imagined future experiences. That is what I want from my writing. I want to inspire educators to consider the possibilities that are yet to exist, for each student, in a world where hegemonic pressures loom in ways that make it incredibly challenging to push back against.

Math and physical sciences always made sense to me. I think they made sense because of positivism, which is prevalent in the fields—the scientific method that ensures reproducibility and the myth of perfection at first attempt (see Hersh, 1991). Because of their positivistic axiomatic relationships, math and physical science in high school and early post-secondary mad sense to me. These simplistic and positivistic relationships made it easier to be prescriptive as a student and as an educator. The perception of necessary algorithmical processes made it so that we can do step-by-step analysis, teaching, and consultations. These relationships work, until they don't. They only fail if we care about all students and believe that all students can learn, understand, and know. These understandings ignored who the students were and their affective knowledge. Instead seeing math and physical science in that way cause a lock step teaching method and fictitious learning that was no more than memorization—not transferable and not personalized.

Statistical data is important to understand but applying it in the right way is much more important. Applying effect size measurements that seek to address a large population as if a large sample where an individual is an educational misnomer. Any one student cannot be understood as a statistic. As I progressed in my career, I realized that relationships needed to be the place so that we as teachers can mediate learning outcomes through our ethical relationality (Ermine, 2007) of and with students. Outcome planning, preparation, and attainment through our understanding of students is contrary to prominent pedagogical understanding where students are expected to produce and repeat a singular or multiple acceptable evidence.

This shift is not profound or cutting edge until I reflexively consider my intentions and values. Through the process of this personal history self-study, I have reaffirmed that relationships are fundamental to learning. I remember many things about my career as a learner but most of what I remember is how I felt within the learning environment. It was the care and commitment that effective teachers showed that motivated me. It was the respect and the trust that was always present regardless of the situation, for all students. It was the knowledge and responsibility which motivated me to persevere even through struggles that I remember most.

The shifts in my pedagogy and practices over time best fit within a pedagogy of love. A name/action/feeling which we seem to intentionally remove from Albertan curriculum. Is it fear of the term? Is it fear of the perception? I believe it is because the word love is incredibly challenging to define and is used in many different even inappropriate ways. I believe that the English language limits us by forcing the naming of a word such as love as static rather than relational and animate (Kimmerer, 2013). Through the remainder of this chapter, I will discuss the findings of my personal history self-study that has sought to uncover some of the possible causes of changes in my pedagogy to away for a formulaic dehumanized approach towards one which hinges on relationality, hope, and possibility. A pedagogy of love.

Architects by Rise Against (Foreword)

Are there no fighters left here anymore?
Are we the generation we've been waiting for?
Are we patiently burning, waiting to be saved?

Our heroes are icons that mellow with age,
Following rules that they once disobeyed.
They're now being led when they used to lead the way.

Do you still believe in all the things
That you stood by before?
I hope they're on the front lines
Or at home keeping score.
Do you care to be the layer of the bricks that seal your fate?
Or would you rather be the architect
Of what we might create?
(Principe & Barnes, 2011, para. 1-3)

Diffuse Reflections: September 2021

Here I am in a completely different context than just a few months ago. We all know that the world changed as of mid-March, 2020 in Canada, and earlier in other parts of the world. Due to the threat of COVID-19 many things that we took for granted need to be reconsidered and re-evaluated. Public spaces, restaurants, school, and education as a whole need to be reconsidered. What is deemed necessity is dictated and moderated through Draconian measures put in place to support the general health and well-being of humanity.

In the context of electromagnetic theory, there is a distinction between two of the ways that light may reflect off a surface. Specular reflection is used to describe the way in which we expect images to appear within a planar mirror—neat, obvious, and predictable. Diffuse reflection, in contrast, produces a distorted image like the one that can be observed in a lake with ripples—messy, imperfect, and occasionally shocking. These two types of reflection serve as excellent metaphors for educational paradigms, with specular representing the way many would have you believe education should or could be—simple, positivistic, and mechanistic as critiqued by Steinberg and Kincheloe (2018), and Hargreaves and Ainscow (2015). While diffuse is a more adequate representation for education—enmeshed, interrelated, and correlated but unpredictable (Biesta, 2013; Doll, 1993; Jones, 2013). Another applicable representation of these reflection metaphors is to the ways that I recall my own experiences. Specular for the simple way that I would like to remember my past or diffuse for the (inter)(intra)related way that I may not ever fully know. Through the challenging and occasionally emotional recursive process of personal history self-study I interrogated who I am as an educator and why I feel that I have shifted so far in my practices and pedagogy. The metaphors that I hold for education, learning, knowing, and knowledge have shifted greatly over time and all of them involve decentering teachers and books as the only keepers of knowledge while placing students and their understanding at the center of all decisions.

Emergent Themes and Entailments

In the following sections I share the major themes that have emerged as the result of reflexive dialogical engagements. Through engaging in a critical personal history self-study with critical friends, I have been afforded an opportunity to better understand myself, my identity, and my pedagogy.

Personal history self-study has proven to be an incredibly useful means to engage in the reflexive activity of getting to the heart of what I believe and what I understand. Personal history self-study has helped me build stronger relationships with critical friends whose kindness and care have fostered my own deepened and more coherent personal understandings. However, self-study has been incredibly painful and joyous at times. It has drawn out memories that I had forgotten, instances that I had recalled differently—perhaps fictitiously recollected. I'm convinced that self-study is a powerful way to get to the heart of what I know but it does have its costs. Self-study has allowed me to identify and interrogate the power dynamics that exist in my work and allows me to bring others into the dialogue, furthering my internal dialogue. Self-study has helped me understand the evolution of my practice, the evolution of my pedagogy, and the evolution of my core beliefs. It helped to draw out some of the events, dialogues, and interactions that have brought me to this moment.

While there were many things that I could have drawn out in the process of this self-study, the one thing that kept coming up was bell hooks' (2001, 2003) definition of love as a combination of care, commitment, knowledge, responsibility, respect, and trust. Love was and is the major theme of my transformations as an educator, a leader, and as a person. Love has been my driver and catalyst for change. As Clingan (2015) suggests "in some way everything that is written about change, transformation, or justice is about love" (n.p.). Through its necessity of trust, responsibility, care, and commitment, love drives me to be a better person, parent, partner, educator, and human. Through its necessity of knowledge, and respect, love motivates me to consider the history, present, and future of all things that I live. So, how do I understand my life as an educator and where does love fit?

In the next few sections I use Samaras et al., (2004)'s three properties of self-study: 1) self-knowing and forming—and reforming—a professional identity; 2) modeling and testing effective reflection; and, 3) pushing the boundaries of teaching. (p. 913), to share what I have come to understand about myself and the educational possibilities that I envision. Additionally, I will share how some of my metaphorical understandings of education have changed over time in each of the contexts.

Love

To understand education, one must love it or care deeply about learning, and accept it as a legitimate process for growth and change. To accept education as it is, however, is to betray it. To accept education without betraying it, you must love it for those values that show what it might become. (Battiste, 2013, p. 190)

bell hooks (2001, 2003) defines love as a combination of care, commitment, knowledge, responsibility, respect, and trust, where all of these characteristics work (inter/intra)-dependently. Love is enacted and not simply a feeling (hooks, 2000). Weber (2017) states that:

> Love is not a pleasant feeling, but the practical principle of creative enlivenment. This principle describes the way in which living communities on this planet—groups of cells, organisms, ecosystems, tribes, families—find their own identities while also fostering the relationship that they have with others and with the system surrounding them. (p. 6)

hooks (2010) suggests that there is a reciprocity between all members of the loving classroom community.

> The loving classroom is one in which students are taught, both in the presence and practice of the teacher, that critical exchange can take place without diminishing anyone's spirit…. While teachers in their leadership are in the best position to create a climate of love in the classroom, students have the power to share their love of learning in a manner that can ignite sparks in a teacher that may be emotionally disengaged. No matter the direction from which love emerges in the classroom, it transforms. (p. 162)

Love, which is often intentionally removed from the curriculum is what should be considered part of the human curriculum (Clingan, 2015), and love is inherently interwoven within strong professional relationships and care. Darder (2017) suggests that "greater possibilities for school and social transformations can be realized" (p. 96) when we engage in dialogue where love is at the heart of the work. It is with a deep sense of care, commitment, knowledge, responsibility, respect, and trust—love—that I engage with students every day and that is how I can critically reflect on the possibilities of change that may be enacted through self-study.

Love as I have known it has become a romanticized version of what I am trying to get across in my writing. While I understand passion and romantic love to exist, through the process of this critical personal history self-study my intention has been, at least partially, to trouble common perceptions of what love can mean and in turn what pedagogies of love can afford. From the bell hooks definition of love, I have come to better understand that love can provide room us. I now better understand that when we have loving relationships and in turn enact pedagogies of love there is space for failure, struggles, mistakes, and hurt to evolve and grow into something stronger and more robust, something different that could not have been there before. It is the enactment of pedagogies of love that allows for personal and collective growth.

We exist in multiple moments—now, through a lens of the affective, storied, fictitious past—while understanding "that the person we are always becoming is being shaped" (Seidel, 2014, p. 145). As educators of generations of young people, it is our moral and ethical responsibility to (re)consider our understandings of classroom pedagogies with a sense of urgency and humility— a refocus on a shift toward pedagogies of love. Dialogical pedagogies may allow for tensions of individual understandings to be juxtaposed through ethical relationality. Clingan (2015) shares:

> If we humans move beyond the feeling and the fears about love, stretch our minds past our wondering about love, and take our greatest philosophies and thoughts about love to a consistent practical application, that we will see healthier communities that are filled with and sustained by love. (n.p.)

Love and wisdom

> *Wisdom's a gift, but you trade it for youth*
> *(Koenig et al., 2013, 2:39-2:42).*

There are numerous definitions and metaphors for wisdom, many of them are related to age and experience; however, these understanding seem to be rooted in love. Cozolino (2013) suggests that wisdom is the way in which intelligences are brought harmoniously together—the synergy of the heart and mind. Staudinger (1999) suggests that those who appear to be wiser are "creative, endorse a judicial, and nonconservative cognitive style, furthermore, are open to new experiences and show personal growth, as well as having been exposed to existential life events and/or to certain professional settings" (p. 660). Wisdom appears to be related and embodied within a life of love, a comprehensive experience and outlook, empathetic and kind outlook, and attitude to and for others (Cozolino, 2013), and resiliency for personal responsibility towards growth-focused solution attainment (Holliday & Chandler, 1986). Wisdom is not simply gained through experience, time, or existence.

Becoming wise appears to be more about an openness to hearing, witnessing, and envisioning the possible. "While knowledge gives you the capacity to understand what you are doing, wisdom helps you to attain correct, prudent, and just application of that knowledge" (Cozolino, 2013, p. 209). Wisdom may be about experiencing and then better knowing how to respond in the future. Richard Wagamese (2016) poetically suggests:

> Knowledge is not wisdom. But wisdom is knowledge in action. I have lived most of my years immersed in the culture of books. I command a lot of facts. I comprehend a lot of concepts. That does not make me wise or even intelligent. It just indicates what I have memorized. But when I activate those facts and concepts to find the greatest, grandest version of myself, and then use them to move towards that vision, I begin the process of wisdom. The most essential question to ask myself is not "What do I think about this?" but rather "How do I feel about this?" In such simplicity is greatness made possible for an individual, society and human family. (p. 130)

Wisdom can be about supporting others through one's own experiences. "Wise individuals also seem to transcend the notion of a single correct perspective, remain open to new learning, and recognize the inescapable distortions inherent in one's own perspectives" (Cozolino, 2013, p. 211). For me best practices rhetorics have evolved to better practices and then to wiser practices—always evolving. For "it is in the journey that one becomes wise" (Wagamese, 2019, p. 51).

I now understand wisdom, at least in the context of educational relevance as embodied pedagogical dampening. Dampening, much like the act of reducing oscillations in the physical sciences when considered through the lens of educational experience, allows me to remain focused on my pedagogical purpose and vision. Wisdom helps us to know that we are on a correct path to supporting learners even if we cannot see that path laid out before us. Wisdom can provide us faith in the pedagogy of love as a means to trust and commit to supporting all learners. Wisdom requires a deep understanding of specific pedagogical content so that we may be better able to listen to our students through writings and dialogues and truly hear their intentions and not just our own—seeking to hear contextual meanings and not searching for faults.

Love as radical listening

> *School adults and youth find their practices bound by epistemological, ontological and axiological schemas that prioritize social efficiency and sameness, maintain the status quo, and squelch out possibilities for social change. (Winchell, Kress, & Tobin, 2016, p.105)*

Radical listening is an idea that I had not been familiar with prior to my research; however, I feel that without knowing it I had shifted towards the use of radical listening as part of my pedagogy throughout my teaching and administrative career. Without radical listening as described by Winchell et al. (2016), I am not certain that love within an educational context can exist.

According to them "radical listening involves consciously valuing others by attempting to hear what the speaker is saying for the meaning he or she intends, rather than the meaning the listener interprets through his/her own view of the world" (p. 101). In their work they reflect on the teachings of Joe Kincheloe (see Kincheloe, 2008b, 2005a) where they specify that in order to gain critical consciousness; first, one must recognize that (1) knowledge is contextual and can never be separated from the knower; (2) the ways of knowing we reward as educators reflects what we value; and (3) in order to re-envision our understanding of the world must listen in value what others have to say about the world specifically those with understandings that vary from our own (Winchell et al., 2016).

Radical listening requires teachers to have an incredibly in-depth understanding of their content knowledge and curriculum because they must hear the students' voice and understandings to engage in dialogue in order to help guide the pathways of their learning—teachers must enact wisdom to know when not to interject and simply (or not so simply) listen. Radical listening allows for shifts in power dynamics within the classroom. Radical listening requires the teacher to be placed into a position where they are not the knower of all information. Decentering the teacher and their power within a classroom space is an act of love and is atypical of what most Albertan pedagogical practises and teaching metaphors necessitate. Winchell et al. (2016) challenge that "it is possible that what might arise from being reflexively aware of radical listening included learning from other, setting aside one's own standpoints, and messing with axiology by intentionally dis-privileging cherished values" (p. 102). This is an ontological, epistemological, and axiological shift in what the classroom typically looks like. I suspect that radical listening is not incorporated in the classrooms typically because of the shift in power where outcomes and lesson plans cannot be met in traditional ways—ways where we can be certain of students achieving every outcome in an acceptable manner.

Radical listening requires that we acknowledge the complexity in the messiness of the affective side of humanity within the classroom. We must acknowledge what students bring with them and what students' lives look like outside of the classroom while incorporating their knowledges into the work that we do every day. Radical listening demands that we acknowledge the *beautiful risk of education* (Biesta, 2013), whereby we truly acknowledge that students are autonomous beings with motivations and preconceived understandings. Radical listening requires the teacher to be brave and trust in the process of learning where knowledge is not some fixed understanding but rather how we negotiate the way we see the world.

Radical listening allows for moving away from singularity of understanding towards a multiplicity of ways to make sense of ideas and concepts. Radical listening requires teachers, in a loving manner, to encourage dialogue as a means for transformations. It shifts the privilege of hearing towards the student's intention when speaking. Conguergood (2003) suggests "metaphors of sound privilege temporal process, proximity, and incorporation. Listening is an interiorizing experience, a gathering together, a drawing in" (p. 357). This does not mean that everything is acceptable, but what it does mean is that within a classroom where love as radical listening is prioritized, students do not always need to look towards the teacher as the person who holds the acceptable representations of knowledge; rather, the teacher would actively engage in dialogue with learners looking to discuss and occasionally draw out roots of understandings. Creating opportunities for dialogue may allow all students to grow to love the process of learning supported collectively through its struggles and challenges. Freire (1996) suggests that:

> Dialogue cannot exist, however, in the absence of profound love. The naming of the world, which is an act of creation and re-creation, is not possible if it is not infused with love. Love is at the same time the foundation of dialogue and dialogue itself. (p. 70)

It is important to recognize that radical listening does not require that students run classrooms, but what it does is allows for students to have a voice within a classroom. It is a decentering of the teacher's power, but still allows for direction and focus, when necessary, by a caring and loving teacher who is a guide rather than the center of attention. This is a shift in a metaphorical understanding of teaching itself. This is an ancillary understanding of teaching— teachers as guides walking and learning beside students.

For teachers just beginning to consider the idea of radical listening, it does not entail a huge shift in practice. Teachers could attempt to enter into dialogues by welcoming students, cautious to not impose their own personal standpoint (Tobin, 2009), and then begin by listening for what students are trying to say, what their intention was and is, and to ask for clarification when they are not certain. Teachers can simply use language like "what I hear you saying is," or "is this what you were saying?" These are great opportunities to member check—to celebrate and guide while acknowledging that knowledge is not singular and is negotiated while being certain not to make negotiated knowledge unsubsumable. This process can help students uncover understandings and misconceptions in a kind way.

Radical listening is a pedagogy of love when enacted within the classroom where teachers trust in the learning process and in turn commit to all learners based on the relationships that they have with them and the knowledge they have of those learners. This commitment to learners respects them as individuals within the classroom community. Ultimately, "radical listening is thus prismatic and transformative, involving multiplicities of culture, experiences, and self, which works to counter the monochromatic epistemologies and ontologies that are prized by social efficiency and puts forth as "universal truths" for all humanity" (Winchell et al., 2016, p. 106).

Love as relationality

Relationality and trust are intimately interconnected and therefore, for me, are enactments of love. As Kovach (2017) suggests, "relationality is a set of values; relationship is the action" (p. 223). When we celebrate differences, we enact love. As we recognize the complexity of relationality when working with other humans, we begin to see that there can be no singular way to understand, learn, or see. This does not mean that we cannot come to the same conclusions, but helps us to recognize the infinite pathways we can take towards understandings.

By understanding the tentative state of flux (Kovach, 2017) in which we exist, we may challenge our perception of reality. We do not always have one-to-one means to map our paradigms and worldviews to those of others in order to communicate effectively. And, this is not a problem if we engage in a loving manner, if our pedagogy, planning, and practices will allow for the respect and knowledge of others. It is the recognition and valuing of difference as the place where we can incorporate an ethical relationality (Ermine, 2007) that can allow for dialogues that seek understanding rather than power. Seeing our paradigms as possibly incommensurable to those of others, we can then begin to consider different vantage points. It is this comfort with the discomfort of relationality that will allow us "not to extrapolate but rather to seek situational understanding" (Kovach, 2017, p. 221).

Because we have listened to only one story for so long—the hegemonic voice of the Albertan educational ethic—we are at risk of having only one story that can be heard. To disrupt this singular, isolated, voice, Thomas King (2003) suggests, "Want a different ethic? Tell a different story" (p. 164).

Therefore, we must consider ethical relationality to better communicate across our historical and cultural differences. Dwayne Donald (2009) posits:

> Ethical relationality is an ecological understanding of human relationality that does not deny difference, but rather seeks to more deeply understand how our different histories and experiences position us in relation to each other. This form of relationality is ethical because it does not overlook or invisiblize the particular historical, cultural, and social contexts from which a particular person understands and experiences living in the world. It puts these considerations at the forefront of engagements across frontiers of difference. (p. 6)

As educators interested in shifting classroom practices and pedagogies towards those of love, it is imperative that relationality is at the forefront of our work. Ethical relationality and dialogue are entangled in a way that are co-implicit. We must seek to understand, hear, and radically listen to value student knowledges and thoughts. Freire (1996) advises a necessity for true dialogue:

> Founding itself upon love, humility, and faith, dialogue becomes a horizontal relationship of which mutual trust between the dialoguers is the logical consequence. It would be a contradiction in terms if dialogue—loving, humble, and full of faith—did not produce this climate of mutual trust, which leads the dialoguers into ever closer partnership in the naming of the world. (p. 72)

Todd (2003) imagines that by "engaging in a speaker-listener encounter creates a potential space for hope for both the speaker and the listener. This is a hope that signals trust in new forms of knowledge and new forms of relationality" (p. 125), and may support the emergence of a non-binary, non-dichotomous understanding of a world that was not conceivable through previously static, linearly dependent paradigms.

Professional relationships within a classroom focused on pedagogies of love require care, commitment, knowledge, responsibility, respect, and trust, and it is the actions that the teacher carries out and the ethic that they uphold and foster within the space that fosters relationality. This relationality may allow for safe spaces for students to take greater risks which can allow for learning opportunities that transcend learning outcomes occasioning for transference to other knowledges. A pedagogy of love is interwoven with relationship and relationality.

Love as an opportunity to change and grow

Author Richard Wagamese (see Wagamese, 2011c, 2014) writes fiction through the lens of love as he looks back and reflects on the choices he has made and pain that these choices may have caused. While neither of these two works are completely autobiographical, they are incredibly indicative of the impacts that all choices educators make on a daily basis can have on students. Richard Wagamese (2016), in an eloquent and incredibly intuitive manner suggests that:

> Love is not always the perfection of moments or the sum of all the shining days—sometimes it's to drift apart, to be broken, to be disassembled by life and living, but always to come back together and to be each other's glue again. Love is an act of life, and we are made more by the living. (p. 151)

There is little doubt that Richard Wagamese was not specifically writing about education; however, if we could consider his intention through the lens of education there could be a fruitful dialogue. In this sense, love could be the willingness for an educator that embodies care, commitment, knowledge, responsibility, respect, and trust to risk focusing on growth and change, mediated through their understanding of their students. To risk moving away from tradition and consider the possible. The risk of the possible is the fear of the unknown—a deviation from the safety of prescription and construction. The enactment of pedagogies of love occurs through transformations to perceived static understandings of knowledge. It is through transformations and growth that we enact pedagogies of love (Clingan, 2010). The benefit is that students may come to recognize that risk creates the opportunity for great, new, and better outcomes. Classrooms focused on pedagogies of love could provide the opportunity for the betterment of all. For, "If the world is saved, it will not be saved by old minds with new programs but by new minds with no programs at all" (Quinn, 1999, p. 8).

Love can, in the most peculiar ways, allow us to be who we can be. When we truly love someone, we are allowing them to achieve the potential that they were intended to have (Wagamese, 2019). Love is the belief that we can change. Love is the belief that we can grow. In education, love manifests as a faith in the possible—the possible afforded in an unknown future supporting learners. For educators, love in this sense means that we must be able to let go of the belief that we can always know our impact on student learning and learning outcomes. I suggest that this faith in supporting learners is much bigger than outcomes; it is much bigger than solely meeting achievable, objective, quantifiable goals.

Faith in the possibility of education requires relationality, a faith in the relationships with others. Specifically, love in education requires critical caring teacher colleagues that could help to perturbate our own practice. Moving us toward disequilibrium, challenging the status quo, and allowing for us to better support the specific context of all learners in our care. Educational leaders can afford this type of faith in the possible by providing time for teachers to come together, work, and engage in discourse regarding specifics of student learning. As teachers build strong relationships with each other, the enactment of their reflexivity would be the shift from a comfortable equilibrium and of a certainty around what education is and can look like. These enactments require structures of safety that will allow for teachers to push each other and their certainty of knowledge. This trusting relationality enacted through pedagogies of love is emotional work. It requires teachers to live in a state of discomfort which I acknowledge could increase anxiety and stress levels; however, over time may help educators to understand that learning is an uncertain and transformative adventure that is more like an ongoing experiment than it is a linear pathway to the attainment of a static body of knowledge. In education, love is beauty—the beauty of learner perseverance supported in the Brownian stumble towards coherence.

Taking up this research as a criticalist is paradigmatically unsettling because our work requires that we interrogate the political structures and systems that exist in education and how those structures and systems impact learners. The reason why this interrogation is unsettling is that much of our personal teaching paradigms were constructed based on the belief that there was the best way to educate, to learn, to know, and to understand—a static monologue of the world. The decentering of a single way of knowing will likely be unsettling for pedagogies that place positivistic beliefs at the core of their understandings. Taking up this work as part of a critical self-study can be emotionally "traumatic" because it requires one to look at their work and personalize how they have embodied hegemonic structures and systems throughout their entire life. It will also challenge perceptions and metaphors of teaching and how the enactments have impacted students, whether that be positive or negative.

While my practice has evolved over time—I cannot even picture myself teaching the way I had when I first started—there are certain threads of my lifetime's paradigmatic evolution that still exist. When I look back at my teaching experience with students, I often fear that I have negatively impacted learners. Sure, there are times when you get positive feedback from students about how we made their lives better; however, the thing I fear the most is the silent voices that don't share or provide feedback about how I may have not served them well. I could have done better if I had known better. This seems to be the impossible task of education—, through our experience and gained wisdom we get better at what we do often through the daily experiment that we were enacting. But it is my faith in the ability of education and more specifically pedagogies of love to support what was previously considered to be unachievable that keeps me working to grow and learn.

Love as the beginnings of decolonizing education

> *Modern educational thought finds actual human consciousness too messy to be studied, which may account for why youth get the facts but not the discussion of what their own purpose is within the life in which they are submersed. (Battiste, 2013, p. 31)*

I identify as a white, middle-class, currently-able-bodied, male—the privileged of the privileged. But what should I be doing with this understanding? When I look back in consideration of my life and the pathways that I chose, I can't help but feel that many of these paths were never options for others. I am well educated and English language proficient in a culture that equates such proficiencies with status. What are the opportunities that I was afforded through nothing more than a genetic and situational luxury? Did I truly enact and earn my current lot in life?

I was a successful student; it is not surprising that I became an educator. I am one of the ones for whom the Eurocentric colonized curriculum was effective. The education that I received was a typically positivistic, singularly hegemonic truth taught through the narrative of racist myths (Donald, 2009). The strength of this education was its neat, orderly, truth-focused absolutism, a form of cognitive imperialism (Battiste, 2013) that assumes that the dominant understanding of the world is the only possible, correct, and privileged knowledge which is perpetuated throughout Western society (Apple, 1998). Unfortunately, cognitive imperialism will never be an adequate enactment of curriculum, "it denies the fact that human beings have their own ways of being and thinking, their own reasons and motivations" (Biesta, 2013, p. 3).

As a school administrator, I learn daily about the struggles and tragedies that some students, entrusted to me, must survive in their home lives: the violence, the addictions, the abuses. Often, our walls are the only safe place that students have known; education for many of these students is the vocation of love. I was never in need of these supports. This was not my reality, nor, I would guess, was it the reality of most of the predominantly middle-classed white educators that currently greet students in classrooms. Typically, these are caring, wonderful, compassionate, empathetic people that do the best they know how given their privileged experiences. Educators that live and die by the successes and failures of their beloved students and enact the only curriculum that they know—a colonized, familiar, static body of knowledge. The singular colonized vision of success sets up a dichotomous reality of have or have-not, success or failure, normal or deviant. These binaries are the embodied and enacted politics of Eurocentric education and its curriculum. Marie Battiste (2013) suggests that "the modern educational system was created to maintain the identity, language, and culture of a colonial society" (p. 30). So, we have caring people doing the best that they know how while perpetuating a continued convergence towards "a single intellectual and spiritual modality" (Davis, 2009, p. 192). How can we disrupt these static colonial paradigms? How can I help to decolonize curriculum? I now truly believe that decolonizing the curriculum is an enactment of love.

What is decolonization of curriculum and education? Perhaps decolonization of curriculum begins with a recognition of the possible, the awakening to the multiplicity of epistemologies, an awareness of the divergence of thought that just may be one of many truths. Decolonizing curriculum and classroom spaces is about honouring and celebrating relationality, truly listening to students and de-centering knowledge structures—it is about enacting a pedagogy of love. Not a state of "epistemological relativism" (McLaren, 2001, p. 701), rather the understanding by educators that all learners come to us with their own world curricula (Lessard et al., 2015) with their own preconceptions and understandings.

As educators begin to imagine the possibilities of a decolonized curriculum, they will begin to become comfortable with the uncomfortable—the complex, divergent, messy, and self-sustaining nature of a curriculum that can be empowering to all learners. Educators enacting a decolonized curriculum could facilitate students' divergence of thought towards the not yet imagined.

To be responsive and responsible to students we must keep being reflexive regarding what we understand to be the purpose of school. This question is time dependent, culturally specific, and societally determined. Is the purpose of school to prepare students for the workforce? Is it to improve the well-being of the individual, or perhaps for the improvement of the collective good? Could it be that the purpose of school is to facilitate a divergent understanding, what is known by "rendering the familiar strange" (Davis et al., 2008, p. 28), or to "create [the] conditions for the human capacity for knowing and learning to become expanded" (Sumara & Davis, 2013, p. 326)?

The colonized, white, Eurocentric curriculum, one which ignores all but the dominant culture's truths, is based on driving students towards the attainment of discrete, measurable, quantifiable objectives; predetermined objectives that are already fully understood—a dead body of knowledge. Popham (2013) suggests, "for objectives to function effectively in instructional and evaluation situations, they must be stated in terms of measurable learner behavior" (p. 95). In this curricular context students must be objectively measured. This implies that a specific—often identical—expected behavior has already been anticipated as a measure of the successful attainment of the objective regardless of who the learner may be. Treating each of these learners as identical does not allow for the divergence of thought or variation of the process. In this vision of education, deviation is easy to deal with—it indicates a failure on the part of the student. This "desire to make education strong, secure, predictable, and risk-free" (Biesta, 2013, p. 3) is deeply entrenched within the positivist Albertan curricular paradigm. The safety that comes with this risk-free, reductionist belief about education and students may satisfy conservative stakeholders and government officials, but it does not recognize learners for who they are—complex organisms that act both independently and as part of larger collectives. "It denies the fact that human beings have their own ways of being and thinking, their own reasons and motivations" (p. 3).

From my perspective, a fundamental flaw with the prescribed measurement of privileged educational objectives is that we ignore the infinite possible objectives that are not necessarily measurable. Eisner (2013) cautions that "imposing logical requirements upon the process because they are desirable for assessing the product is, to my mind, an error" (pp. 113-114). Present Eurocentric curricula instead turns to objectives that can be quantified or at least be measured in some manner. "[This] overriding emphasis on quantification and measurement reinforces the belief that aspects of our world that can be quantified are more important than those that cannot" (Baker as cited in Renert, 2011, p. 24). Privileging only these readily measurable, Eurocentrically biased, objectives ensures a curricular mismatch between learners and objectives—learners may not find education engaging or liberating.

To change education—to make it inclusive and empowering for all learners—we must recognize the complexity of learners and their lives. We e must understand that all learners come with their own affective histories, aspirations, motivations, desires, and goals. We can acknowledge students and their need when we enact and embody pedagogies of love which include relationships, empathy, and compassion. Decolonizing the curriculum "depends crucially on the extent which we believe that education is not just about the reproduction of what already exists but is genuinely interested in the ways in which new beginnings and new beginners can come into the world" (Biesta, 2013, p. 4). By rejecting patriarchy and recognizing the multiplicity of epistemologies, we may begin to shift education towards a decolonized curriculum, one that affords hope and opportunity to emancipate all learners—a curriculum of love.

I focus my thoughts on an Albertan curriculum—its history and its plausible future—through a theoretical lens guided by an understanding of the complexity of ecological sensibilities and critical pedagogies. I write as a white male with a great deal of public and private school teaching experience, within a wide variety of cultures. As the result of my formal Western Canadian education and teaching experiences, I am deeply influenced by the physical sciences and the dominance of the successes that positivism has provided these fields since their inceptions. However, I see that the authority of these fields is the likely cause of the implicit belief that humans could somehow engineer a better world. The increasingly apparent negative impacts on the Earth leave me striving to break from this worldview in the hope of finding alternatives—an expanded view of my reality. I look to focus on alternative epistemologies and Indigenous knowledges while recognizing that humanity has achieved many notable successes within the existing paradigm. I cautiously use the term "successes" because of the tenuous current social and environmental state of the world. I hope to relay alternative epistemologies that will allow for a divergence of thought and understanding that can subsume prior pedagogies and schemas. It is by changing definitions from the constraints of singulars to multiplicities: literacy to literacies, knowledge to knowledges, and the possible to possibilities that may allow for the decolonization of curriculum, one which will support increased empathy and allow for coherence of understandings for all learners.

I believe that the incorporation of pedagogies of love in education fosters student empowerment. Empowering students would shift educational priorities from learner passivity to learner action and engagement. Students will be empowered by reading the world and reading the word (Freire, 1996). When the authentic word is mediated by the student's world, a student's reality can be transformed. Through the action-reflection process of praxis, learners can be empowered and in turn can transform their world (Freire, 1996). School is the place for praxis to be fostered. Pedagogies of love may foster emancipatory classroom spaces that "offers the space for change, invention, spontaneous shifts, that can serve as a catalyst" (hooks, 1994, p. 11)—a catalyst for hope, opportunity, and empowerment. Renert (2011) suggests, "since school is a social institution situated at the intersection between present society and the promise of what society may become, educators are more likely to succeed in their work with messages of hope and possibility" (p. 25). To nurture hope, opportunity, and empowerment for all students, education should be decolonized. In order to decolonize education, we recognize that education and teaching are always political acts and are more complex than often recognized—there can be no generic understanding of knowledges or experiences. The affective experiences of learners influence all aspects of present and future lenses; therefore, education and educators must be cognizant of the coherence of the multiplicity of learners' world-curricula (Lessard et al., 2015).

What kind of school do we dream of for our children? We are long past the adequacy of a Tylerian school system that ignores community, treats students as identical automatous inputs, and reduces curriculum to an optimizable object (Tyler, 1949). The production line of education is insufficient; we are no longer preparing students for a defined future. Schools that do not recognize the classroom as a complex adaptive system (Davis et al., 2008, 2015) can no longer be considered effective given that these prior models were "mainly formulated during the simpler conditions of the nineteenth century" (Bobbit, 2013, p. 11)—simpler in all aspects including: pedagogical necessity, population diversity, and societal complexity. We need to be aware that "any inherited system, good for its time, when held to after its day, hampers social progress" (p. 11).

School must be a place that recognizes the multiplicity of literacies and the multiplicity of narratives, one that rejects the singular understandings of colonial education, one that nurtures students' aspirations and strengths, one that is supported by masters of their craft—the embodiment of wisdom and servitude—that facilitate for the empowerment of *all* learners. School must recognize the increasing rate of social, technological, and cultural change. I want my children to thrive and to love education through engagement—not as a cliché, but rather through a *place based* (Gruenewald, 2003), environmentally conscious, inclusive education—one with high standards for all. This education needs to be experiential—an education that recognizes "that our experience is always incomplete" (Greene, 2013, p. 137). An education that requires all students to employ a productive struggle fostered by caring people who facilitate for the coherence of learners' understandings to further their individual levels of comprehension. Not to meet quotas or agendas, rather to better themselves and society, for "education… is a process of living and not a preparation for future living" (Dewey, 2013, p. 35).

Thomas Hobbes's *state of nature* theory is one of the roots for the vision of the Western, Eurocentric model of colonized education (Youngblood, 2000). This "state of nature remains the prime assumption of modernity, a cognitive vantage point from which European colonialists carry out experiments in cognitive modelling and engineering that inform and justify modern Eurocentric scholarship and systemic colonization" (p. 11). The result of this vision is that colonized education supports a movement away from a *savage* state to that of an enlightened singular acceptable state (Youngblood, 2000). These deeply entrenched normalized beliefs embedded in white, racist, dominant culture have made it so that all other cultures can be justifiably oppressed. Battiste (2013) argues that educational theory supports the notion that humans are a product of the "culture and motivation and interest stemming from those structures the society creates." As a result, "the modern educational system was created to maintain the identity, language, and culture of a colonial society" (p. 30). A white colonial society is a social construct (Battiste, 2013); however, the authority, privilege, and hegemonic influences of this construct have immense effects on normalized culture (Apple, 1998; Kincheloe & Steinberg, 1998), and impact all that exists in the geographic region that these dominant societies reach.

My discussion of colonial curriculum refers to the enactment of any form of *cognitive imperialism*. According to Battiste (2013), when "knowledge is omitted or ignored in the schools and a Eurocentric foundation is advanced to the exclusion of other knowledges and languages, these are conditions that define an experience of cognitive imperialism" (p. 26). These conditions are assumed within many Albertan classrooms and are the pedagogical foundations for logic-based, linearly progressing teaching. Linearity in teaching implies linearity in learning—such that there is a pre-defined logical process by which students build on prior understanding to achieve a totality of discrete conceptual understanding. The correct pathway that students are to follow is defined by the teacher's lesson design relative to objectives, where the end goal is already known and fully understood and ready to be assessed. This assessment determines if an adequate measurement of a student's understanding had been achieved. Negative feedback of students towards a predetermined end goal ensures convergence of thought as the result of an Albertan curricula.

Given the linear nature of this perceived learning process, all understandings should be built on prior knowledges—fundamental ideas are taken as given, not to be negotiated, and are known as absolute cultural truths. This is foundational to building metaphors of education—not inherently bad, but occasionally inadequate and improperly associated. Kurt Gödel proved that all ideas that are logic based are fundamentally destined to exist in a paradoxical reality. Gödel's Incompleteness Theorem outlines a contradiction in all proofs that occurs as the result of an inherent paradox. It showed that for every theory there must be an infinite number of statements that may be true but are unprovable axiomatic statements (Kleene, 1967). In the case of a colonized curriculum, these axioms include all of the privileged knowledges that make up the students' prior understandings as well as all of the knowledges that are part of their intentionally excluded null curriculum (Eisner, 1985). This enactment of cognitive imperialism ensures that any student whose culture is not part of the hegemonic norm would be destined to failure because of an irreconcilable incoherence between their school curriculum-making world and their familial curriculum-making world (Lessard et al., 2015). This fragile tower of student's understanding, contingent on all of the logical building blocks of knowledge fitting together in the correct order at the correct time with the student's prior learning, makes it likely that incoherence will cause this logic structure to collapse.

Current enactments of education embody the belief that students and classrooms can be viewed through a positivistic lens as independent variables—able to be isolated and tested—ignoring the complex interconnectivity of change agents. This is a troubling view. Renert (2011) posits, "since the enlightenment, the way humans conceive of the world has been guided by the reductionist scientific paradigm, which maintains that complicated systems can be disassembled and reassembled at will" (p. 23). In the 17th, 18th, and 19th Centuries, the physical sciences were dominated by the successes of the Bacon and Newtonian style of experimentation. These *safe*, quantitative, *legitimate* research methods were readily adopted and served to support a scientific movement in the relatively new field of educational research. In

1918, Bobbit (2013) stated, "the technique of the scientific method is at present being developed for every important aspect of education. Experimental laboratories and schools are discovering accurate methods of measuring and evaluating different types of educational processes" (p. 12). Eisner (1997), when discussing the legitimacy of quantitative data, suggests that "not all forms of data representation have been considered legitimate in the context of research" (p. 5) which supported the intensive drive to quantify educational research data, and "is based on the fundamental misunderstanding of what education is about and a fundamental misunderstanding of what makes education 'work'" (Biesta, 2013, p. 3). As a result of this misrepresentation of the physical sciences, students and classrooms have been treated as variables. They are controllable and manipulatable, having causal relationships. These problems could be conveniently considered those of *simplicity* (Weaver, 1948), which perpetuate the belief of a colonized curriculum whereby all students can be considered identical variables.

A shift in inertia away from a simplistic, predictable, strong, safe, and quantifiable view of education (Biesta, 2013) can be an enactment of love, recognizing that the persistent view of students as *controllable variables* has never been adequate. While it has been fruitful for the physical sciences to operate in a positivist realm, the biological sciences and medical sciences have found little use for positivist problem solving because of the insignificant nature of the problems that could be solved by these means. In education, students and classrooms are not *simply* related. A fundamental flaw in the positivist, colonized curricula is that we only value what we can measure. Alternatively, to view students "not as a complex machine but as a growing organism" (Eisner, 2013, p. 110), while complex, unpredictable, and full of risk is a much more relevant and sufficient view (Biesta, 2013). Recognizing that students and classrooms are "living things [is] more likely to present situations in which a half-dozen, or even several dozen quantities are all varying simultaneously, and in subtly interconnected ways" (Weaver, 1948, p. 536) requiring a completely different paradigm for curricula and research—one focused on quantitative research and narratives.

The dominant belief of a dichotomous society—where Eurocentric culture and beliefs are correct, and all others are inferior—negates the plethora of possible alternative epistemologies. Little Bear (2000) posits, "no matter how dominant a worldview is, there are always other ways of interpreting the world. Different ways of interpreting the world are manifest through different cultures, which are often in opposition to one another" (p. 77). Because dominant culture is the culture that has instituted and maintained a colonized curriculum, it is this same culture that must undergo a transformation in understanding, lens, and pedagogy to decolonize the curriculum. Society's beliefs are a result of the way they think; conversely, the manner in which they think is the direct result of their beliefs (Nisbett, 2003). Therefore, divergent thinking by the dominant culture is required for the decolonization of education—an acceptance of a broader and more sustainable understanding of worldviews.

Decolonizing the curriculum is a process, a process that Battiste (2013) suggests is a "transdisciplinary quest to balance European and Indigenous ways of knowing" (p. 95). While discussing similar decolonization processes, Smith (1999/2012) states that this "does not mean and has not meant a total rejection of all theory and research or Western knowledge. Rather, it is about centering our concerns and world views from our own perspective and for our own purposes" (p. 41). It is not as a complete rejection of the oppressive norm, but rather a divergent transformation that subsumes current pedagogical beliefs—a transformation that incorporates and values alternative epistemologies and worldviews. Decolonizing curriculum and classrooms require teachers to enact pedagogies of love whereby they accept students for who they are and interpret outcomes through their knowledges of the students.

Ermine (2007) suggests the facilitation of *ethical spaces* for praxis that will allow societies with disparate worldviews to "face each other across historical divides, deconstruct their shared pasts, and engage critically with the realization that their present and future are similarly tied together" (Donald, 2009, p. 5). It is this *third space* (Bhahba, 1990) that represents the confluence of potentially opposing knowledge systems that will allow for effective, conscious, ethical communication. "The [ethical] space offers a venue to step out of our allegiances, to detach from the cages of our mental worlds and assume a position where human-to-human dialogue can occur" (Ermine, 2007, p. 202). For teachers, this dialogue represents intensive professional and personal unlearning and relearning. It will not be an instantaneous accumulation of applicable facts; but rather, it will represent the beginning of a journey towards pedagogical transformation—a transformation that will make education a space of inclusivity for all learners. For students, this will represent the continued growth and expansion of their understandings of their personal and collective worldviews, toward a worldview that is more divergently inclusive than that of any previous generation. For these ethical spaces to occur, it is imperative that schools "help to develop an appreciation in the child of the struggle of past generations for progress and liberty, and thereby develop a respect for every truth that aims the human race" (Goldman, 2012, p. 6).

Davis and Sumara (2007) propose that "teaching is more about a conscientious participation in expanding the space of the possible by creating the conditions for the emergence of the not-yet-imaginable" (p. 64). This space of the not-yet-imaginable must include, recognize, and value alternative epistemologies. This is no easy task for educators. They can only exist in their own ever-evolving paradigm while being open to all others. This is not to create a framework for *anything-goes* logic, but rather to open possibilities for culturally, situationally, and contextually relevant curricula. Perhaps then, the decolonization of education is about seeing education for what it can be—to afford hope for *all* learners through the embodiment of pedagogies of love.

A decolonization of curriculum allows for an opening up of possibilities, affording hope, creating opportunity, and empowering learners can only happen through the decolonization of the curriculum. For Little Bear (2000) "One of the problems with colonialism is that it tries to maintain a singular social order by means of force and law, suppressing the diversity of human worldviews" (p. 77). The risk of decolonizing education is that society will recognize the complexity that exists—complexity that is divergent, messy, and self-sustaining. By valuing the multiplicity of epistemologies, education may become more inclusive of all learners—supporting coherence of world-curricula (Lessard et al., 2015) and fostering acceptance of diverse worldviews. Effective, empathetic teachers will be the embodiment of this decolonized curriculum. Guided by their wisdom, they will facilitate the students' divergence of thought.

The work, according to Greene (2013), for "teachers is to stimulate an awareness of the questionable, to aid in the identification of the thematically relevant, to beckon beyond the everyday" (p. 138). As educators, our everyday must be spent realizing and normalizing decolonization, together. Shifting practices and pedagogies to ones that emphasize possibility and love. Colonized curriculum and education with their singular focus and monochromatic understandings are proving to be dangerously limited and risk creating a convergent specialist society—unprepared for change and destined for failure and devoid of love. It is the work of brave educators as guides to delve into the unknown of the not yet imagined working alongside students to make these changes possible.

Margaret Mead spoke of her singular fear that, as we drift toward a more homogenous world, we are laying the foundations of a blandly amorphous and singularly generic modern culture that will have no rivals. The entire imagination of humanity, she feared, might be confined within the limit of a single intellectual and spiritual modality. Her nightmare was the possibility was that we might wake up one day and not even know what had been lost. (Davis, 2009, p. 192)

Love as an Evolution of Leadership Possibilities

The intention of this book was never to illuminate the various types or theoretical stances and entailments of leadership models, nor was it to discuss at any length the chronological lineage of theories. I understand the field of educational leadership comes with its own language and definitions such as authentic leadership (Luthans & Avolio, 2003; Avolio & Gardner, 2005), transformative leadership (Shields, 2016; Leithwood, 2010), sustainable leadership (Hargreaves & Fink, 2004), and servant leadership (Patterson, 2003) just to name a few. The purpose was not to interrogate leadership but rather to interrogate myself. The reason that I have chosen to focus on regenerative leadership in this section is simply because the language and characteristics of this particular leadership model fit well within what I have come to better understand through the process of this personal history self-study.

As an administrator for the last six years, having witnessed the actions of school administrators throughout my entire career, I have noticed a range of characteristics that administrators tend to embody. Table 7 is a summary of four of the groups of characteristics that Hutchins and Storm (2019) argue have been dichotomized through the process of reductionist leadership practices and policies since the time of Enlightenment. These practices have been woven into current business and education leadership practices as the result of the prominence of the positivistic and scientific methods-based accountabilities. See table 7 below for a summary of characteristics and traits that can be associated with reductionist and regenerative leadership.

Table 7. Binaries Associated with Some Leadership Characteristics by Category as Adapted from Hutchins and Storm (2019)

	Binaries Associated With Some Leadership Characteristics	
	More Reductionist	More Regenerative
Gendered	• Masculine • Personal needs • Competition • Assertive • Protective • Goal-Oriented • Rational • Independence • Mono-task • Bias for action	• Feminine • Compassion towards others • Collaborative • Receptive • Nurturing • Relationship-oriented • Intuitive • Interdependence • Multi-task • Bias for flow
Brain Hemisphered	• Left Dominant • You vs. me • Linear • Causal • Reducible • Structure and order • Polarization	• Right Dominant • Unification • Systemic • Relational • Holistic • Creativity • Seeing through tensions
Inner/Outer Separation	• Outer • Rational objectivism of self • Disconnection from emotions • Reductionism	• Inner • Knowledge of self • Connected to emotion • Holism
Human Nature Separation	• Dominance over the environment • Commodification	• Interconnection

It is not my intention to perpetuate binaries; however, for the purpose of the table it is challenging to represent it in any other way. I suggest that we see each of these traits as a continuum which could allow for movement in either direction depending on context. The point that Hutchins and Storm (2019) work to emphasize is that the reductionistic simplification of clean and neat, competitive, and objective, predictable, and obtainable models of leadership have passed their time of effectiveness. They argue that through enacting regenerative leadership, school leaders can remove these imposed binaries and begin to recognize the school as a messy interconnected complex adaptive system.

The Internet provides many examples, gifs, and schematics of what leadership can mean, but I attempt to define my thoughts on these ideas in the context of education. Hutchins and Storm (2019) suggest that one of the major differences between reductionist leadership and *regenerative leadership* is the recognition and enactments of a logic of life which include: systems thinking, systemic awareness, and ecosystems awareness. Table 8 describes some of the characteristics of each of the three logics of life.

Table 8. Logic of Life Descriptors and Characteristics as Adapted from Hutchins and Storm (2019)

Logic of Life	Characteristics
Systems Thinking	• Shifting away from mechanistic understandings • Seeing a system as irreducible and cannot be described in parts • Seeing processes as interrelated • "Systems thinking is a process that takes place at the head level" (Hutchins & Storm, 2019, p. 66) • Pattern recognition • Flux and dynamics rather than stasis
Systemic Awareness	• People in a system are interconnected in a dynamic way including: knowledge, energy, and feedback • Cultural mediated relationships and culture, where each culture is subtly different in each context (non-transferable between location) • Requires reflexivity • The history of the organization is embodied in the culture including past trauma • Holistic connection: body, mind, and heart

Logic of Life	Characteristics
Ecosystems Awareness	• Recognition of the nested systems in which we are apart • Interconnection to all life: animate and inanimate • Attuned to nature • Spiritually aware

While these terms are slightly different from some of the language that I have used throughout this book, I feel that Hutchins and Storm (2019) are proposing a similar evolution to education. Clingan (2010) suggests that all languages that are focused on systemic evolutions or transformations are enactments of love; therefore, school leaders shifting towards regenerative leadership are undergoing a shift towards pedagogies of love whether aware or not. Table 9 outlines the shifts that could be occurring as indicators of school leaders as they begin to embody regenerative leadership/logic of life characteristics.

Table 9. Shifts From Past Logic Towards a Regenerative Leadership/Logic of Life as Adapted from Hutchins and Storm (2019)

Shifts	
From Reductionist Leadership	Towards Regenerative Leadership
• Mechanistic • Linear • Cause-and Effect • Ego/Left Hemisphere • Masculine • Outer Focus	• Interconnected • Systems Thinking • Left-Right Hemisphere Integration • Relational Awareness • Open Mind • Systemic Awareness • Inner-outer Integration • Masculine-Feminine Integration • Embodied Participatory Awareness • Open Heart • Ecosystemic Awareness • Human-Nature Integration • Living Systems Field • Open Will

One may notice that I have come full circle from Table 1 where I discussed the shifts in educational leadership. In the next section I describe what I understand to be enabling constraints within the context of Alberta regarding the implementation of the TQS and LQS. Each of these documents, by which teachers and school leaders are evaluated, has its root in the shifts listed in Table 1 and in turn shares some traits with Table 9.

Reductionist leaders focus on the simple organizational structures that can increase efficiency and effectiveness of practice, while regenerative leaders, as I am defining them, look to unify, amplify, and create opportunities. Reductionist leaders ensure that the work that is done is quantifiable, outcome-focused, and reducible. A reductionist leader's work requires that employees are seen as mechanistic and they fall into mechanistic structures and can be optimized in order to better perform tasks. In the context of education this will be like a focus on better classroom management through multistep process, better teaching as the result of better lesson planning, and the guise of better knowing your children through building better assessments—over-learning simple skills only because they are commensurable.

Focusing on traits and practises that can be quantified and optimized ensures that we will ignore the ones that are incommensurable. By focusing on those discrete pieces of data—the measurement of simplicity—some practises can be improved. I understand why we focus on those pieces of information and that is because we can better those aspects of education with a small input to the system, but do those impacts really matter? This reductionist metaphor of educational leadership is built on a consumerism business model which is also tied to economic growth and profit. Based on those models there must be assurances that goals are met, and stakeholders are increasing profit share, evidenced through quantifiable metrics and data.

Regenerative leadership requires the enactment and embodiment of pedagogies of love: care, commitment, knowledge, responsibility, respect, and trust. As I have shared throughout this book and in accordance with Hutchins and Storm (2019) regenerative leadership:

> requires great courage to relinquish the methods and modes of the old amid increasing volatility and uncertainty…. It's about becoming more creative, more authentic, more purposeful, more compassionate, more in tune with life within us and all around us. It's simply becoming more human. (p. 71)

An Alberta Specific Example: LQS and TQS— Constraints and Impacts

The newly developed LQS (Alberta Education, 2017a) was officially adopted as an evaluative standard for practicing administrators within Alberta as of September 2019 (College of Alberta School Superintendents, 2018; Alberta Education, 2018b). As such, the competencies of: Fostering Effective Relationships, Modelling Commitment to Professional Learning, Embodying Visionary Leadership, Leading a Learning Community, Supporting the Application of Foundational Knowledge about First Nations, Métis and Inuit, Providing Instructional Leadership, Developing Leadership Capacity, Managing School Operations and Resources, and Understanding and Responding to the Larger Societal Context and their indicators will be used as measures for administrator growth (Alberta Education, 2017a).

In Alberta, administrators are members of the Alberta Teachers Association (ATA), as a result they are now obligated to meet the evaluative standards of the new Teaching Qulaity Standard (TQS) (Alberta Education, 2017c) as well. The competencies that teachers are evaluated relative to include: Fostering Effective Relationships, Engaging in Career-Long Learning, Demonstrating a Professional Body of Knowledge, Establishing Inclusive Learning Environments, Applying Foundational Knowledge about First Nations, Métis and Inuit, and Adhering to Legal Frameworks and Policies. As one may notice the TQS and LQS share competencies that use parallel language and the descriptors are similar with the exception that the LQS reference a responsibility to students, teacher, and community and the TQS is limited to student and community relationships. The intention behind this language will become obvious in the following paragraphs but will certainly make it so that educational leaders can actively, collaboratively, and co-implicitly support teachers in their professional learning and growth.

According to Adams (2016), "the practices of school leaders comprise the second highest impact on student learning" (p. 6), the first being the pedagogies and practices of the teacher. However, administrators can positively impact classroom didactics and pedagogies through their management and instructional leadership (Robinson et al., 2008; Seashore Louis et al., 2010). Instructional leadership has changed over time from an exclusive focus on the principal dictating learning agendas towards a new intention of distributed leadership (Hallinger, 2010). Robinson et al. (2008) are adamant that transforming teacher practice requires leaders to learn alongside teaching staff. These shifts have changed throughout a similar timeline from an evaluation documentation of Alberta teachers towards that of a growth framework. Some of these changes can be shown when a comparison of Alberta Education (1997) and Alberta Education (2017c) are considered. Positivistic and reductionistic language permeated the previous iteration of the TQS document and a much more open and less prescriptive angle appears to have been taken in its subsequent iteration. At the time of the initial construction of this accountability document the language used was prominent within the context of Albertan education and schooling and its associated metaphors (Davis et al., 2015). And while this language was an adequate means to hold teachers to high professional standards of accountability, over time these standards have become inadequate.

Bedard and Mombourquette (2016, 2015) suggest that there have been several major evolutions in the expectations and roles of leadership within Alberta schools. These evolutions are reflected within the changes of language and focus of the new TQS and LQS. An openness to emergent possibility is ever more obvious through reading these documents whereby one can possibly envision the competencies as affordances to support increased conceptual understandings (Deleuze & Guattari, 1994; Stern et al., 2017). Whether they will be enacted in ways that afford for divergence is yet to be determined.

These thoughts and transformations align well with the Findings (actions required) and Recommendations (for increasing adaptive learning capacity) of and for Effective High School Redesign Implementation as Adapted from Friesen et al. (2015) in Table 2 and the Foundational Principles of High School Redesign and Indicators as Adapted from Alberta Education (2018a) which are supported by highly regarded and reputable research.

· 5 ·
HOW DO I CONTINUE? GIVEN WHAT I UNDERSTAND.

In this chapter, I share some of my concluding thoughts, possible impacts, and future considerations. As shared previously, the process of engaging in a critical personal history self-study has been emotionally taxing, I would suggest that it has impacted my relationships. However, the process has been incredibly fruitful in bringing to light my life history and experiences and how I have evolved as an educator-turned-administrator to better understand the infinitude of divergent possibilities in education.

I was Jaded: Conclusions

I was jaded by the bureaucratic infringements of people who claim to remember the ways that their deceased educational experiences hindered or helped them work to control the future experiences of youth through stagnant pedagogies. Either way, these memories help to keep education stuck within a torpid paradigm. How do we meet teachers, parents, and stakeholders where they are at, to help them see divergent possibilities for education?

I have been successful as a primary, secondary student, and post-secondary student because of the nature of safe prescriptive pedagogies and assessment practices. All of which have had the singular goal of simplistic outcome attainment. I could reproduce the already well known dominant hegemonic knowledge. Whether it was labs, proofs, or assignments, I was successful because I was able to recognize and understand what my teachers and professors wanted me to know and could predict what they expected to see as evidence of understanding. I struggled to find success in my writing. I struggled to follow prescribed paths: five paragraph formats, keyhole entries, thesis statement, and summative conclusions. I find it impossible to write that way, I generally refuse to read anything that is written that way. That type of writing and literature presents as trite and boring to me.

My frustrations and joys, failures and successes, and passions and disappointments in my own personal educational experiences served as an impetus for much of my reflexivity in this self-study. In my first year of education, I had a professor who mentioned that, as a generality, if education students are not the children of teachers, they enter education for one of two reasons: they loved their personal experiences or they feel that there should be a better way to do things. I fit into both categories. I had many caring, loving, passionate teachers throughout my career as a student and also have several I could use as nonexamples. However, it was not the people, as much as the structures and culture of Western Canadian education that pushed me to consider possibilities for change within education. I see the embodiment of pedagogies of love in education as a way to better support all learners.

I am Grateful: Discussions

I am grateful for the divergent learning experiences that I have had throughout my lifetime. I can't help but question whether or not I earned all of these opportunities. As I reflect on the opportunities afforded to me, I am convinced that I worked hard and met and exceeded expectations consistently, however, I can't help but wonder if I was the "right" person for career advancement due to the privilege of my gender, outward physical appearance, and any other characteristics that were desired rather than my qualifications. Were the expectations the same for all? Was I allowed leniency due to my privilege? I know that the majority of Western Canadian educators are female but the majority of Western Canadian educational leaders, including administrators, are male. This doesn't surprise me; however, I am troubled and left wondering what it is that I can do to facilitate a change in the imbalance. I will keep asking. I will continue as a criticalist to challenge the political structures that exist in education.

I am more confident and able to better advocate for the educational needs of students. I love education for what it might become (Battiste, 2013). I love the opportunities that an inclusive education may afford for all learners. How do we support educators, parents, and communities to better understand alternatives to what was known? How do I create opportunities for growth and change? How do I make it possible to push back against deeply entrenched historical educational structures and pedagogies? How do I maintain the courage to move forward into the messiness that is the uncertainty of school as complex adaptive systems with ecological sensibilities and help others see them as possibilities too?

I am Hopeful: Possibilities and Future Considerations

I believe that education may open possibilities for that which has yet to be imagined. By (re)considering learning as an ongoing evolutionary process occurring within the complex entanglement of interactions within collective learning communities, dialogical pedagogies of critical thinking may be enacted. As Joe Kincheloe (2008a) suggested, pedagogies of love are essential to educational change and intimately connected to critical pedagogy because, "critical pedagogy wants to connect education to that feeling, to embolden teachers and students to act in ways that make a difference, and to push humans to new levels of social and cognitive achievement previously deemed impossible" (p. 4).

Through this critical and reflexive personal history self-study I have identified the themes that I feel define my current identity-in-progress as an educator and administrator. Over my life, my paradigm has evolved from a passive, positivistic, predetermined recognition of the world towards that of an ecological, caring, relational, and interconnected world-in-flux—a symbiotic world where the human and more-than-human world are irreducibly enmeshed. I feel that if educators and administrators can reconsider their understandings of education through a sense of wholeness, embodying pedagogies of love, education may well become the catalyst for societal growth and change. The following major themes were drawn out and illuminated through the process of self-study: 1) love and wisdom; 2) love as radical listening; 3) love as relationality; 4) love as an opportunity to grow and change; 5) love as the beginnings of decolonizing education; and, 6) love as an evolution of leadership possibilities. Each of the themes require the embodiment of care, commitment, knowledge, responsibility, respect, and trust by educators and administrators in order to afford for emergent possibilities for students.

By looking further than statistics and effect sizes and considering the wholeness of learners and their affective experiences, education may possibly achieve substantially more than it was ever intended to do. "When we act from love the results transform for the good. With love our laws can change, our systems can change, and we can in fact begin to heal the world" (Clingan, 2015, n.p.). Life preparation—a known, predictable life—is no longer the purpose or intention of school. Pedagogies that serve as a catalyst for social awareness and social change should and can be the hope and possibility of education.

I feel that personal history self-study is a reflexive growth opportunity for all administrator and educators that are willing, who are brave enough to undertake the emotional turmoil that can emerge through its undertaking. I have no doubt that self-study can support for personal growth and change and in turn may occasion for community and cultural evolution as well. If educators and administrators could envision alternative possibilities for education the opportunities for students could be amazing.

Rochelle Brock (2005) suggests that "when education targets wholeness of being and spirituality, individual and collective transformation happens" (p. 94). Education that prioritizes the ethical engagement of students and respects their academic well-being while winning their hearts and souls will prove to support social change. bell hooks (1994) is adamant that by teaching "in a manner that respects and cares for the souls of our students is essential if we are to provide the necessary conditions where learning can most deeply and intimately begin" (p. 13). By departing from the safety of the oppressive rational ideal of an already imagined future we can consider a future through a pedagogy of love that is not yet imagined—a place of the possible.

What I Have Come to Understand: Thoughts Around the Non-Generalizable

I have previously mentioned that the intention of this critical personal history self-study was to interrogate myself. The intention was never to bring a level of generalizability to my understanding or the ways in which I have come to understand education in Alberta or Western Canada. I acknowledge that there are likely themes that readers will connect with, moments where they feel challenged, moments where they disagree, and I hope, an occasional epiphany. This bricolage of coming to better know myself, my paradigms, and my beliefs has drawn on the entirety of my personal history and has caused many instances of personal turmoil, and... I am tired. But what was the point?

Themes from my story were exposed, and while I know the subjectivity of self-knowledge research could allow for different themes to emerge at different times in my life, the focus on love and on pedagogies of love is what most vividly speaks to me in this moment. I discussed love in a similar manner to bell hooks and hope to have illuminated that I believe critical and valuable work in education is somewhere within the confluence of criticality and complexity. I better understand all things are interconnected. It is this ecological sensibility I envision as a direct challenge to the reductionistic, fictitious simplification of classroom dynamics. A challenge to pedagogies that conjure a singular, formulaic, prescriptive, and safe understanding of living classrooms—classrooms that are in fact ever-emergent, continually adapting, and divergently redundant. These are spaces of the possible, of the not-yet-imagined, they can be the fertile locations of growth and change.

Pedagogies of love can be understood as more than the embodiment of romantic notions of the word. Pedagogies of love enact relationality: blending care, commitment, knowledge, responsibility, respect, and trust. Ever-evolving and situational, we take these pedagogies as tentative. Incorporating pedagogies of love into the classroom will not ensure appropriate attainment of specific scholastic outcomes; however, I question that positivistic approach applied in social environments such as classrooms will not ensure specific outcome attainment. It has been easier to ignore outliers, to define them as inadequate. The pedagogies of love focused on care, commitment, knowledge, responsibility, respect, and trust can help students to understand that being human is important. These pedagogies can help students to redefine what it *can* mean to be human and may support a broader awareness of how we are not disconnected from the more-than-human world. These pedagogies can facilitate students in understanding *who they are is as important as what they understand;* and what can be shown on assessments. This shift in pedagogy presents the possibility for students to better understand their interconnection and inherent responsibilities to others and the world. Students can be motivated to see the beauty of the messiness that is the enmeshed complexity of society and the human and more-than-human worlds. A pedagogy of love can lead our students to see, hear, and feel how we are deeply in need of all these worlds.

Enacting a pedagogy of love can allow for an equitable and socially just education which allows for stronger, collaborative, and kind relationships. Kahn and Kellner (2008) suggest that "education, at its best, provides the symbolic and cultural capital that empowers people to survive and prosper in an increasingly complex and changing world and the resources to produce a more cooperative, democratic, egalitarian, and just society" (p. 25). I believe we deserve this society.

Architects (Afterword)

Yeah, we still believe in all the things
That we stood by before,
And after everything we've seen here
Maybe even more.
I know we're not the only ones
And we were not the first.
And unapologetically
We stand behind each word.
(Principe & Barnes, 2011, para. 10)

GLOSSARY

Collectivity: The interactions and relationships associated with a group of individuals. According to Davis, Sumara, and Luce-Kapler (2015) collectivity can be associated with crowdsourcing. Collectivity allows "a group of people to be more intelligent than the most intelligent person in the group" (p. 133).

Competency: An interrelated set of knowledges and understandings that evolve over time and are contextual in nature.

Complexity: Complexity tends to be a counter-narrative to that of simplicity—a movement away from Newtonian cause and effect. According to Doll (1993) complexity "is viewed from an evolutionary perspective where, over time, hierarchical systems or networks of organization develop that cannot be reduced from one to the other" (p. 65).

Complex Adaptive System: According to Jones (2013) there are three key distinct characteristics of complex adaptive systems. All complex adaptive systems are self-maintaining (dependent on the environment but able to regulate within it), self-renewing (constantly and recursively reimagining or replenishing), and self-transcending (able to adapt, be creative to survive through change). These systems are related and interconnected, non-linear, and chaotic. As they evolve, a "new order is a natural outcome" (Morgan, 2006, p. 252) which I understand to be applicable to classroom dynamics.

Conceptual Metaphor: "A grounded, interference-preserving cross-domain mapping—a neural mechanism that allows us to use the inferential structure of one conceptual domain to reason about another" (Lakoff & Nunez, 2000, p. 6). For example, the metaphor of time as currency, allows us to consider "wasting time" or "time well spent." Metaphors are the embodiment of experience in the world. Whenever we interact with complex ideas, we apply multiple metaphorical understandings. Lakoff and Nunez (2000) continue to share that:

> A conceptual metaphor is a cognitive mechanism for allowing us to reason about one kind of thing as if it were another. This means that metaphor is not simply a linguistic phenomenon, a mere figure of speech. Rather, it is a cognitive mechanism that belongs in the realm of thought. (p. 6)

Ecological Sensibility: The term "ecological" is often understood as in relation to nature, which is to say, separate from humans. When I use the term "ecological," I hope to create an alternative narrative of connection. I understand ecological sensibility in a similar manner to Sumara, Davis, and Laidlaw (2001) when they suggest that discussions of connections

> are not simply matters of environmental awareness. They are, rather, indicative of a certain ecological sensibility. To draw an important distinction, *environmental* and *ecological* announce two very different ways of thinking. "Environmental" implies a separation of observer and observed, as it points to concerns with surroundings. In contrast, "ecological" is about relationships, with particular attention to the complex co-evolutions of humans and the more-than-human world (Abram, 1996, p. 148). (p. 148)

Connection is meant as a social complex construct and is not intended to establish binaries; in fact, I hope to evoke an awareness of how everything and everyone are somehow enmeshed in a complex web. Leroy Little Bear (2000) suggests that an Aboriginal worldview recognizes that "all things are animate, imbued with spirit, and in constant motion" (p. 77). This is a powerful notion that affords a revisioning of connection that is contrary to colonial constructs. For, "if everything is animate, then everything has spirit and knowledge. If everything has spirit and knowledge, then all are like me. If all are like me, then all are my relations" (Little Bear, 2000, p. 78). I will occasionally use (inter/intra)connected throughout the following work to illustrate an ecological sensibility.

To extend on Sumara et al. (2001), I have a similar understanding to Weber (2017) I will use ecological sensibility as a term that describes the ecology of a living, dynamic relationship where everything is considered to be co-implicit, co-impactful, and co-evolutionary. When discussing Indigenous education Cajete (1994) shares:

> The environment was not something separate from their lives, but was the context, the set of relationships, that connected everything. An understanding of ecology was not something apart from themselves or outside their intellectual reality, but the center and generator of self-understanding. (p. 87)

Through all of this I hope to share that I see ecological sensibility as my understanding of the blurred lines of "mutually affective relationships" (Sumara et al., 2001, p. 150) of complex interactions.

GLOSSARY 131

Educational Rationalism: According to Gereluk et al. (2016) educational rationalism requires that students play an active role in their learning. Davis (2004) posits that educational rationalism is often misinterpreted as rationalism. He suggests that, as defined by Piaget, educational rationalism is not the passive receiving of knowledge from a more informed teacher.

Enlightenment: The era generally accepted to span from the 16th to the 19th century (Baudrillard, 1987; Gereluk et al., 2016). During this time science and the scientific method became popularized and the prominence of rational criticisms of dominant established traditions came into question (Rorty, 1984). Enlightenment was the beginning of the era where positivism and a desire to understand the world emerged. Habermas and Ben-Habib (1981) claim that "Enlightenment philosophers wanted to utilize this accumulation of specialized culture for the enrichment of everyday life, that is to say, for the rational organization of everyday social life" (p. 9).

Identity: Can be understood as the characteristics of one's personality. However, this definition risks being understood as static. As Sumara and Luce-Kapler posit, "although we acknowledge the importance of interpreting narrations of lived experiences, we believe these activities often entrench an understanding of teaching identity as something that hangs, suspended, between teaching and non-teaching experiences" (Sumara & Luce-Kapler, 1996, p. 67). Britzman (1991) suggests that teaching identity is as much about taking up the ways in which others see the self. She shares:

For those who leave this world to enter teacher education, their first culture shock maywell occur with the realization of the overwhelming complexity of the teacher's work and the myriad ways this complexity is masked and misunderstood. But what occurs as well is the startling idea that the taking up of an identity means suppressing aspects of the self. So at first glance, becoming a teacher may mean becoming someone you are not. (p. 4)

I have come to understand teaching identity as something that we never fully achieve (Allan, 2017) and is always negotiated and relational (Dewey, 2013).

Indicators: Alberta Education (2017a) defines indicators as "actions that are likely to lead to the achievement of a competency and which, together with the competency, are measurable and observable" (p. 3).

Paradigm: According to Shawn Wilson (2008) a paradigm is a label "used to identify sets of underlying beliefs or assumptions upon which research is based" (p. 33). These axiomatic and fundamental understandings held by researchers impact what they see, hear, and feel—influencing what they know and believe. Wilson goes on to suggest that "as paradigms deal with beliefs and assumptions about reality, they are based upon theory and are intrinsically value laden" (p. 33).

Personal History Self-Study: Self-study research exists in the confluence of biography and history (Bullough & Pinnegar, 2001), whereby the researcher situates themselves inside the process (Samaras, 2010). Personal history self-study as defined by Samaras et al. (2004) includes both the autobiographical and life-history of the teacher and challenges them to work to improve their practice. Foundational to this personal history self-study research process are the following three possibilities for teaching as defined by Samaras et al. (2004)

1. self-knowing and forming—and reforming—a professional identity;
2. modeling and testing effective reflection; and,
3. pushing the boundaries of teaching. (p. 913)

Perturbation: Pirie and Kieren (1994) make reference to perturbation as that push away from a state of equilibrium. I will tend to use disruption generally synonymously with perturbing or perturbation. In the context of education, they suggest that "the teacher expects children to hold unique and different understandings, reached by different pathways of growth, and these understandings are not achieved states of equilibrium" (p. 40). In a complex adaptive system, movement away from a state of equilibrium causes the system to adapt and reconfigure. This metaphorical understanding of learning fits well within the context of ecological sensibilities associated with learning in social environments with their multiplicities of influences.

Positioning: Positioning, as I am using the term, is a way by which I attempt to help readers understand who I am and what my intentions are. By sharing information about myself I recognize that readers are more likely to trust in the narratives and information that I share. As Kovach (2017) states, "it is not simply about trust in the findings and 'validation of the data'; it is about trust in the relationship" (p. 224). It is important that I attempt to place myself with the context of the study and the work that I am doing through sharing my life experiences.

Positivism: Is the belief in the possibility of a direct possible cause-effect relationship between variables. Through this lens, understandings can be rationally reduced, verified, and logically supported through science. Generalizable laws can be used to determine how society and the world function—the belief that there can be an absolute, verifiable, objective, knowable truth. According to Ortony (1993), "a basic notion of positivism was that reality could be precisely described through the medium of language in a manner that was clear, unambiguous, and, in principle, testable—reality could, and should, be literally describable" (p. 1). Newtonian and Descartian understandings along with scientific methods have become prominent enactments of positivism.

Rationalism: the understanding that actions, opinions, and beliefs should be solely based on logical reasoning. Rationalism is the belief that deduction should be used for all decision-making processes and implies that all knowledge and understandings are innate.

Reification: According to Sfard (1994) reification "is the birth of the metaphor of an ontological object.... Reification is the transition from an operational to a structural embodied schema" (p. 53). Reification can be considered to be the construction of coherent metaphors that can become the basis for understanding (Sfard, 1994).

Relationality: According to Sean Wilson (2008) a researcher's work and its validity are contingent on the relationship that one has with the researcher. He claims that this relationality cannot be disconnected from their work, and "requires that you know a lot more about me before you can begin to understand my work" (p. 12). As Margaret Kovach (2017) states, "it is not simply about trust in the findings and 'validation of the data'; it is about trust in the relationship" (p. 224). She continues by positing that "relationality is a set of values; relationship is the action" (p. 223).

Schema: According to Gereluk et al. (2016), a schema is "a coherent set of beliefs about how some aspect of the world works, which may or may not be true" (p. 49). An example of this could be something like models of atomic structures. For example, prior to Niels Bohr's first quantum atomic model of the atom there were many other iterations which all considered the microscopic properties of the atom to take on properties of the macroscopic world. These schemas, built upon axioms, were later disproven through experimentation and research.

Self-study: Self-study research exists in the confluence of biography and history (Bullough & Pinnegar, 2001), whereby the researcher situates themselves inside the process (Samaras, 2010). Self-study is a recognition of a turn in educational research that acknowledges the intersection of self and other. Self-study is "autobiographical, historical, cultural, and political and takes a thoughtful look at texts read, experiences had, people known and ideas considered" (Hamilton & Pinnegar, 1998, p. 236). While biography and autobiography also attempt to explain and share the story of a person, it is the lack of interrogation and recursion through dialogues that distinguishes self-study from autobiography and biography.

Tacit: Tacit has been used throughout this study and its write-up. I understand tacit to be considered in a similar manner to Davis and Renert (2013b) whereby one of the fundamental differences between the master teacher and the novice teacher is the way that they embody knowledges. A tacit understanding is meant to be one which is taken as understood and embodied in a manner that does not require active engagement or reflection on its meaning. In this context, the master teacher's/administrator's experiences with specific content have led them to enact the enmeshment, overlap, and interconnectivity of multiple metaphors without needing to distinguish between them unlike the novice.

Tentative: Tentative in the context of this book will generally be a belief in the unfinished ways in which I hold understandings. As Steinberg (2012b) suggests that research is tentative in nature which I believe is because the dynamics of relationships are understandings that are always in flux—never finished.

Understanding: That which I have come to know at this time

REFERENCES

Abram, D. (1996). *The spell of the sensuous: Perception and language in a more-than-human world.* Pantheon Books.

Adams, P. (2017). Enacting Alberta school leaders' professional practice competencies: A toolkit by Bedard, G. J., & Mombourquette, C. A. *Canadian Journal of Educational Administration and Policy* (182), 6-8. https://journalhosting.ucalgary.ca/index.php/cjeap/article/view/42065

Alberta Education. (2013, October). *Teaching quality standard applicable to the provision of basic education in Alberta.* https://education.alberta.ca/media/1626523/english-tqs-card-2013_3.pdf

Alberta Education. (2017a). *Leadership quality standard.* https://education.alberta.ca/media/3739621/standardsdoc-lqs-_fa-web-2018-01-17.pdf

Alberta Education. (2017b). *Leadership quality standard competencies.* https://education.alberta.ca/media/3739993/competencies-infograph-lqs-eng-2018-01-19.pdf

Alberta Education. (2017c). *Teaching quality standard.* Retrieved from https://education.alberta.ca/media/3739620/standardsdoc-tqs-_fa-web-2018-01-17.pdf

Alberta Education. (2017d). *Teaching quality standard competencies.* https://education.alberta.ca/media/3739994/competencies-infograph-tqs-eng_print-2018-01-19.pdf

Alberta Education. (2018a). Moving forward with high school redesign. https://www.alberta.ca/moving-forward-with-high-school-redesign.aspx?utm_source=redirector

Alberta Education. (2018b). *Professional practice standards.* https://education.alberta.ca/professional-practice-standards/new-professional-standards/

Alberta Education. (2019). Programs of study. https://www.alberta.ca/programs-of-study.aspx

Alcoff, L. M. (1991). The problem of speaking for Others. *Cultural Critique* (Winter, 1991-1992), 5-32. https://depts.washington.edu/egoline/wordpress/wp-content/uploads/2010/05/Alcoff-Reading.pdf

Allan, S. L. (2017). Borderlands of possibility: Exploring the construction of professional identity with Intern teachers. *In Education, 23*(1), 2-25.

Allbritton, D. W. (1995). When metaphors function as schemas: Some cognitive effects of conceptual metaphors. *Metaphor and Symbol, 10*(1), 33-46.

Anderson, P. M. (2018). The meaning of pedagogy. In J. L. Kincheloe & S. R. Steinberg (Eds.), *Classroom Teaching: An Introduction* (2nd ed., pp. 17-28). Peter Lang.

Aoki, T. (1993). Legitimizing lived curriculum: Towards a landscape of multiplicity. *Journal of Curriculum and Supervision, 8*(3), 255-268.

Aoki, T. (2004). Teaching as in-dwelling between two curriculum worlds (1986/1991). In *Curriculum in a New Key* (pp. 179-186). Routledge.

Apple, M. (1998). Forward. In J. L. Kincheloe, S. R. Steinberg, N. M. Rodriguez, & R. E. Chennault (Eds.), *White reign: Deploying whiteness in America* (pp. ix-xiii). St. Martin's Griffin.

Apple, M. W. (2012). *Knowledge, power, and education: The selected works of Michael W. Apple*. Routledge.

Austin, P. (1996). Gatekeeper or gardener? In search of a metaphor for teacher education. *The Clearing House, 70*(2), 101-102.

Avolio, B. J., & Gardner, W. L. (2005). Authentic leadership development: Getting to the root of positive forms of leadership. *The Leadership Quarterly, 16*(3), 315-338.

Barto, M., & Bedford, A. W. (2013). Henry Giroux: Man on fire. In J. D. Kirylo (Ed.), *A critical pedagogy of resistance: 34 pedagogues we need to know* (pp. 61-64). Sense.

Battiste, M. (2013). *Decolonizing education: Nourishing the learning spirit*. Purich.

Baudrillard, J. (1987). Modernity. *Canadian Journal of Political and Social Theory, 11*(3), 63-72.

Beckers, G., & Hannula, A. (2013). Deborah Britzman: Critical thinker, researcher, psychoanalyst. In J. D. Kirylo (Ed.), *A critical pedagogy of resistance: 34 pedagogues we need to know* (pp. 13-16). Sense.

Bedard, G. J., & Mombourquette, C. P. (2015). Conceptualizing Alberta district leadership practices: A cross-case analysis. *Leadership and Policy in Schools, 14*(2), 233-255.

Bedard, G. J., & Mombourquette, C. P. (2016). *Enacting Alberta School leaders' professional practice competencies: A Toolkit*. FriesenPress.

Bhabha, H. (1990). The third space. In J. Rutherford (Ed.), *Identity: Community, culture, difference* (pp. 207–21). Lawrence and Wishart.

Biesta, G. J. J. (2013). *The beautiful risk of education*. Paradigm.

Bloomberg, L. D., & Volpe, M. (2016). *Completing your qualitative dissertation: A road map from beginning to end* (3rd ed.). Sage.

Bobbitt, F. (2013). Scientific method in curriculum-making. In D. J. Flinders & S. J. Thornton (Eds.), *The curriculum studies reader* (4th ed., pp. 11-18). Routledge.

Bourdieu, P. (1990). *The logic of practice*. Stanford University Press.

Bourdieu, P. (2017). *Outline a theory of practice*. Cambridge University Press (original work published in 1977).

Bovitch, S., Cullimore, Z., Bramwell-Jones, T., Massas, E., & Perun, D. (2011). The educational theory of Noam Chomsky. *New Foundations*. http://www.newfoundations.com/GALLERY/Chomsky.html

Brandon, J., Hanna, P., Morrow, R., Rhyason, K., & Schmold, S. (2013). *The Alberta framework for school system success*. CASS.

Britzman, D. (1986). Cultural myths in the making of a teacher: Biography and social structure in teacher education. *Harvard Educational Review*, 56(4), 442–456.

Britzman, D. (1991). *Practice makes practice: A critical study of learning to teach*. State University of New York Press.

Britzman, D. (2003). *Practice makes practice: A critical study of learning to teach*. SUNY Press.

Britzman, D. (2011). *Freud and education*. Routledge.

Britzman, D. (2013). Between psychoanalysis and pedagogy: Scenes of rapprochement and alienation. *Curriculum Inquiry*, 43(1), 95-117.

Brock, R. (2005). *Sista talk: The personal and the pedagogical* (Vol. 145). Peter Lang.

Bryk, A. S., & Schneider, B. L. (2002). *Trust in schools: A core resource for improvement*. Russell Sage Foundation.

Bullough, R. V. Jr., & Gitlin, A. (1995). *Becoming a student of teaching: Methodologies for exploring self and school context*. Garland Publishing, Inc.

Bullough, R. V. Jr., & Stokes, D. K. (1994). Analyzing personal teaching metaphors in preservice teacher education as a means for encouraging professional development. *American Education Research Journal*, 31(1), 197-224.

Bullough, R. V. Jr., & Pinnegar, S. (2001). Guidelines for quality in autobiographical forms of self-study research. *Educational Researcher*, 30(3), 13-21.

Carspecken, F. P. (2013). *Critical ethnography in educational research: A theoretical and practical guide*. Routledge.

Cajete, G. (1994). Look to the mountain. *Ecology of indigenous education*. Kivaki Press.

Chomsky, N. (1999). *Chomsky on miseducation*. Oxford.

Chubberly, E. P. (1916). *Public school administration*. Houton Mifflin.

Clandinin, D. J. (1995). Still learning to teach. In T. Russell & F. Korthagen (Eds.), *Teachers who teach teachers: Reflections on teacher education* (pp. 25–31). Falmer Press.

Clandinin, D. J., & Connelly, F. M. (1990). Narrative, experience and the study of curriculum. *Cambridge Journal of Education*, 20(3), 241-253.

Clandinin, D. J., & Connelly, M. (2004). Knowledge, narrative and self-study. In *International handbook of self-study of teaching and teacher education practices* (pp. 575-600). Springer, Dordrecht.

Clingan, J. (2010). A pedagogy of love. *Journal of Sustainability Education*, 9.

Cohen, I. B., (2006). *The triumph of numbers: How counting shaped modern life*. W. Norton.

Cohen, L., Manion, L., & Morrison, K. (2011a). The ethics of educational and social research. In L. Cohen, L. Manion & K. Morrison, *Research Methods in Education* (7th ed., pp. 52–77). Routledge.

Cohen, L., Manion, L., & Morrison, K. (2011b). Validity and reliability. In L. Cohen, L. Manion & K. Morrison, *Research Methods in Education* (7th ed., pp. 134–164). Routledge.

College of Alberta School Superintendents. (2018). *Executive summary of supports for implementation of the professional practice standard(s)*. https://cassalberta.ca/wp-content/uploads/2018/11/Supports-for-Implementation-Executive-Summary-.docx

Colonna, S. E., & Nix-Stevenson, D. (2015). Radical love: Love all, serve all. *The International Journal of Critical Pedagogy, 6*(1), 5–25.

Conquergood, D. (1991). Rethinking ethnography: Towards a critical cultural politics. In Y. Lincoln & N. Denzin (eds.), *Turning points in qualitative research: tying knots in a hankerchief* (pp. 351-374).

Cook-Sather, A. (2003). Movements of mind: The matrix, metaphors, and re-imagining education. *Teachers college record, 105*(6), 946-977.

Cozolino, L. (2012). *The social neuroscience of education: Optimizing attachment and learning in the classroom*. WW Norton.

Creswell, J. W., & Creswell, J. D. (2017). *Research design: Qualitative, quantitative, and mixed methods approaches*. Sage.

Cruikshank, J. (2000). *Social life of stories: Narrative and knowledge in the Yukon Territory*. UBC Press.

Darder, A. (2017). *Reinventing Paulo Freire: A pedagogy of love*. Routledge.

Daughenbaugh, L. R., & Shaw, E. L. (2013). Judith Butler: Philosophy of resistance. In J. D. Kirylo (Ed.), *A critical pedagogy of resistance: 34 pedagogues we need to know* (pp. 17-20). Sense.

Davies, B. (2006). Subjectification: The relevance of Butler's analysis for education. *British Journal of Sociology of Education, 27*(4), 245-438. [Special Issue: Troubling Identities: Reflections on Judith Butler's Philosophy for the Sociology of Education].

Davis, B. (2004). *Inventions of teaching: A genealogy*. Lawrence Erlbaum Associates, Inc.

Davis, B., & Renert, M. (2013a). *The math teachers know: Profound understanding of emergent mathematics*. Routledge.

Davis, B., & Renert, M. (2013b). Profound understanding of emergent mathematics: broadening the construct of teachers' disciplinary knowledge. *Educational Studies in Mathematics, 82*(2), 245-265.

Davis, B., & Simmt, E. (2006). Mathematics-for-teaching: An ongoing investigation of the mathematics that teachers (need to) know. *Educational Studies in Mathematics, 61*, 293-319

Davis, B., & Sumara, D. (2007). Complexity science and education: Reconceptualizing the teacher's role in learning. *Interchange, 38*(1), 53–67.

Davis, B., Sumara, D., & D'Amour, L. (2012). Understanding school districts as learning systems: Some lessons from three cases of complex transformation. *Journal of Educational Change, 13*(3), 373-399.

Davis, B., Sumara, D., & Luce-Kapler, R. (2008). *Engaging minds: Changing teaching in complex times*. Routledge.

Davis, B., Sumara, D., & Luce-Kapler, R. (2015). *Engaging minds: Cultures of education and practices of teaching* (3rd ed.). Routledge.

Davis, W. (2009). *The Wayfinders: Why ancient wisdom matters in the modern world*. House of Anansi Press.
Deal, T. E. (2009). Poetical and political leadership. In B. Davies (Ed.), *The essentials of school leadership* (pp. 133–146). Sage.
Deleuze, G., & Guattari, F. (1994). *What is philosophy?* Columbia University Press.
Dei, G. J. S. (2008). Race, schooling, and the education of African youth. *Journal of Black Studies, 38*(3), 346-366.
Dei, G. J. S., & Simmons M. (2018). Indigenous knowledges and the challenge for rethinking conventional educational philosophy. In J. L. Kincheloe & S. R. Steinberg (Eds.), *Classroom teaching: An introduction* (2nd ed., pp. 57-69). Peter Lang.
Dewey, J. (1902). *The child and curriculum*. University of Chicago Press.
Dewey, J. (1915). *The school and society*. University of Chicago Press.
Dewey, J. (1938). *Experience and education*. Touchstone.
Dewey, J. (2013). My pedagogic creed. In D. J. Flinders, & S. J. Thornton (Eds.), *The curriculum studies reader* (4th ed., pp. 33-40). Routledge.
Doll, W. (1993). *A post-modern perspective on curriculum*. Teachers College Press.
Doll, W. (2012). Modes of thought. In *Pragmatism, postmodernism, and complexity theory: The" fascinating Imaginative Realm" of William E. Doll, Jr*. Routledge.
Donald, D. (2009). Forts, curriculum and Indigenous Métissage: Imagining decolonization of Aboriginal-Canadian relations in educational contexts. *First Nations Perspectives, 2*(1), 1-24.
Dweck, C. (2007). *Mindset: The new psychology of success*. Ballantine Books.
Eisner, E. W. (1985). *The educational imagination: On the design and evaluation of school programs* (2nd ed.). Macmillan Publishing Co.
Eisner, E. (1997). The promise and perils of alternative forms of data representation. *Educational Researcher, 26*(6), 4-10.
Eisner, E. W. (2013). Educational objectives—help or hindrance. In D. J. Flinders, & S. J. Thornton (Eds.), *The curriculum studies reader* (4th ed., pp. 315-329). Routledge.
Ellsworth, E. (1997). *Teaching positions: Difference, pedagogy, and the power of address*. Teachers College Press.
Emler, N. (2001). *Self esteem: The costs and causes of low self worth*. Publishing Services.
Erickson, F. (2017). A history of qualitative inquiry in social and education research. In N.K. Denzin & Y.S. Lincoln (Eds.), *The Sage handbook of qualitative research* (5th ed., pp. 36-65). Sage.
Ermine, W. (2007). The ethical space of engagement. *Indigenous Law Journal, 6*(1), 193-203.
Freire, P. (1994). *Pedagogy of hope: Reliving pedagogy of the oppressed*. Bloomsbury.
Freire, P. (1996). *Pedagogy of the oppressed*. Penguin (original work published 1970).
Friesen, S. [@sfriesen]. (2019, January 22). Best practices discourse provides no opportunity for improvement or reimagining otherwise. It also leaves no space for considering the learning. [Tweet]. Twitter. https://twitter.com/sfriesen?lang=en
Fullan, M. (2011). *Choosing the wrong drivers for whole system reform*. http://education.qld.gov.au/projects/educationviews/news-views/2011/nov/talking-point-fullan-101117.html
Fullan, M. (2014). *The principal: Three keys to maximizing impact*. John Wiley & Sons.

Gereluk, D., Martin, C., Maxwell, B., & Norris, T. (2016). *Questioning the classroom: Perspectives on Canadian education*. Oxford University Press.

Goldman, E. (1912). *The social importance of the modern school*. Emma Goldman Papers: Rare Books and Manuscripts Division, New York Public Library.

Goodson, I. (1999). The educational researcher as public intellectual. *British Educational Research Journal, 25*(3), 277-297.

Goodson, I., & Gill, S. (2011). *Narrative pedagogy: Life history and learning* (Vol. 386). Peter Lang.

Giroux, H. A. (1997). *Pedagogy and politics of hope: Theory, culture, and schooling*. Westview Press.

Giroux, H. A. (2011). *On critical pedagogy*. Bloomsbury Publishing USA.

Giroux, H. (2018). *Pedagogy and the politics of hope: Theory, culture, and schooling: A critical reader*. Routledge.

Gómez, J. (2002). Learning communities: When learning in common means school success for all. *MCT, 20*(2), 13-17.

Greene, M. (2013). Curriculum and consciousness. In D. J. Flinders, & S. J. Thornton (Eds.), *The curriculum studies reader* (4th ed., pp. 127-138). Routledge.

Grumet, M. R. (1990). Retrospective: Autobiography and the analysis of educational experience. *Cambridge journal of Education, 20*(3), 321-325.

Gruenewald, D. (2003). The best of both worlds: A critical pedagogy of place. *Educational Researcher, 32*(4), 3-12.

Habermas, J., & Ben-Habib, S. (1981). Modernity versus postmodernity. *New German Critique*, (22), 3-14.

Hallinger, P. (2010). Developing instructional leadership. In B. Davies & M. Burnett (Eds.), *Developing successful leaders* (pp. 61–76). Springer.

Hamilton, M. L., & Pinnegar, S. (1998). Conclusion: The value and promise of self-study. In M. L. Hamilton (Ed.), *Reconceptualizing teaching practice: Self-study in teacher education* (pp. 235-246). Falmer Press.

Hargreaves, A. (2003). *Teaching in the knowledge society: Education in the age of insecurity*. Teachers College Press.

Hargreaves, A., & Ainscow, M. (2015). The top and bottom of leadership and change. *Phi Delta Kappan, 97*(3), 42-48.

Hargreaves, A., & Fink, D. (2004). The seven principles of sustainable leadership. *Educational leadership, 61*(7), 8-13.

Hargreaves, A., & Lowenhaupt, R. (2017). Leading with consistency: How the ends don't always justify the means (and vice versa). In D. Waite and I. Bogotch (Eds.), *The Wiley international handbook of educational leadership* (pp. 63-78). John Wiley & Sons.

Hargreaves, A., & O'Connor, M. T. (2017). Cultures of professional collaboration: their origins and opponents. *Journal of Professional Capital and Community, 2*(2), 74-85.

Hargreaves, A., & O'Connor, M. T. (2018). Solidarity with solidity: The case for collaborative professionalism. *Phi Delta Kappan, 100*(1), 20-24.

Hasebe-Ludt, E., Chamber, C. M, & Leggo, C. (2009). *Life writing and literary métissage as an ethos for our time*. Peter Lang.

Hattie, J. (2011). *Visible learning for teachers: Maximizing impact on learning*. Routledge.

Henderson, J. G., & Gornik, R. (2007). *Transformative curriculum leadership*. Prentice Hall.

Hersh, R. (1991). Mathematics has a front and a back. *Synthese*, 88(2), 127-133.

Hinchman, L. P., & Hinchman, S. (1997). *Memory, identity, community: The idea of narrative in the human sciences*. Suny Press.

Holliday, S. G., & Chandler, M. J. (1986). *Wisdom: Explorations in adult competence*. Karger.

Holt-Reynolds, D. (1991). *Practicing what we teach*: National Center for Research on Teacher Learning, East Lansing, MI. Sponsored by the Office of Educational Research and Improvement (ED), Washington, D. C. Research Report 91-5. ED 337460.

Honig, M. (2012). District central office leadership as teaching: How central office administrators support principals' development as instructional leaders. *Educational Administration Quarterly*, 48, 733–774. doi:10.1177/0013161X12443258

Honig, M., Copland, M., Rainey, L., Lorton, J., & Newton, M. (2010). *Central office transformation for district-wide teaching and learning improvement* (Vol. 46). Professional Media Group, LLC.

hooks, b. (1994). *Teaching to transgress: Education as the practice of freedom*. Routledge.

hooks, b. (2001). *All about love: New visions*. Harper Collins.

hooks, b. (2003). *Teaching community: A pedagogy of hope*. Routledge.

hooks, b. (2010). *Teaching critical thinking: Practical wisdom*. Routledge.

Innes, R. A. (2009). "Wait a Second. Who Are You Anyways?" The Insider/Outsider Debate and American Indian Studies. *American Indian Quarterly*, 33(4), 440-461.

Johnson, M. (1987). *The body in the mind*. The University of Chicago Press.

Jones, T. (2013). Complexity theory. In B. Irby (Ed.), *Handbook of educational theories* (pp. 815-819). Information Age Publishing.

Kahn, R., & Kellner, D. (2008). Paulo Freire and Ivan Illich: Technology, politics and the reconstruction of education. In C.A. Torres & P. Noguera (Eds.), *Social justice education for teachers* (pp. 13-34). Sense Publishers.

Kanu, Y. (2003). Curriculum as cultural practice: Postcolonial imagination. *Journal of the Canadian Association for Curriculum Studies*, 1(1), 67-81.

Kellner, D. (1995). *Media culture: Cultural studies, identity and politics between the modern and postmodern*. Routledge.

Kemmis, S., & McTaggart, R. (1988). *Action research reader*. University Press.

Kimmerer, R. W. (2013). *Braiding sweetgrass: Indigenous wisdom, scientific knowledge, and the teachings of plants*. Milkweed Editions.

Kincheloe, J. L. (2001). Describing the bricolage: Conceptualizing a new rigor in qualitative research. *Qualitative inquiry*, 7(6), 679-692.

Kincheloe, J. L. (2005a). *Critical constructivism primer* (Vol. 2). Peter Lang.

Kincheloe, J. L. (2005b). On to the next level: Continuing the conceptualization of the bricolage. *Qualitative inquiry*, 11(3), 323-350.

Kincheloe, J. L. (2005c). Introduction: Educational psychology—Traversing a treacherous terrain. In J. L. Kincheloe & R. Horn (Eds.), *Educational psychology: An encyclopedia*. Greenwood.

Kincheloe, J. L. (2008a). *Critical pedagogy* (2nd ed.). Peter Lang.

Kincheloe, J. L. (2008b). *Knowledge and critical pedagogy: An introduction* (Vol. 1). Springer Science & Business Media.

Kincheloe, J., & McLaren, P. (1994). *You can't get to the yellow brick road from here*. Routledge.

Kincheloe, J. L., McLaren P., Steinberg S. R., & Monzó L. D. (2017). Critical pedagogy and qualitative research: Moving to the bricolage. In N. K. Denzin & Y. S. Lincoln (Eds.), *The Sage handbook of qualitative research* (5th ed., pp. 235-260). Sage.

Kincheloe, J. L., & Steinberg, S. R. (1998). Addressing the crisis of whiteness: Reconfiguring white identity in a pedagogy of whiteness. In J. L. Kincheloe, S. R. Steinberg, N. M. Rodriguez, & R. E. Chennault (Eds.), *White reign: Deploying whiteness in America* (pp. 3-32). St. Martin's Griffin.

Kincheloe, J. L., & Tobin, K. (2015). The much exaggerated death of positivism. In S. R. Steinberg, & K. Tobin (Eds.), *Doing Educational Research* (pp. 15-32). Brill Sense.

King, S. (2000). *On writing: A memoir of the craft*. Simon and Schuster.

King, T. (2003). *The truth about stories: A native narrative*. Harper Collins.

Kirylo, J. D. (2013). Introduction: Resistance, courage, and action. In J. D. Kirylo (Ed.), *A critical pedagogy of resistance: 34 pedagogues we need to know* (pp. xix-xxvi). Sense.

Kitchen, J. (2005). Looking backward, moving forward: Understanding my narrative as a teacher educator. *Studying Teacher Education, 1*(1), 17-30.

Kleene, S. C. (1967). *Mathematical Logic*. Wiley.

Knapp, M. S., Copland, M., Honig, M., Plecki, M. L., & Portin, B. S. (2010). *Learning-focused leadership and leadership support: Meaning and practice in urban systems*. Center for the Study of Teaching and Policy, University of Washington.

Kobak, R., & Madsen, S. (2008). Disruption in attachment bonds: Implications for theory, research, and critical intervention. In J. Cassidy & P. R. Shaver (Eds.), *Handbook of attachment: Theory research, and clinical applications* (pp. 23-47). The Guilford Press.

Koenig, E., Batmanglij, R., & Gates, D. A. (2013). Step [Song recorded by Vampire Weekend]. On *Modern Vampires of the City*. Universal.

Kovach, M. (2010). *Indigenous methodologies: Characteristics, conversations, and contexts*. University of Toronto Press.

Kovach, M. (2017). Doing Indigenous methodologies: A letter to a research class. In N. K. Denzin & Y. S. Lincoln (Eds.), *The Sage handbook of qualitative research* (5th ed., pp. 214-234). Sage.

Kraehe, A. M. (2015). Sounds of silence: Race and emergent counter-narratives of art teacher identity. *Studies in Art Education, 56*(3), 199-213.

Krammer, D., Mangiardi, R. (2012). The hidden curriculum of schooling: A duoethnographic exploration of what schools teach us about schooling. In J. Norris, R. D. Sawyer, D. Lund (Eds.), *Duoethnography: Dialogical methods for social, health, and educational research* (pp. 41-69). Left Coast Press.

Kuhn, T. S. (1996). *The structure of scientific revolutions*. Chicago University Press.

Kumashiro, K. (2002). Against repetition: Addressing resistance to anti-oppressive change in the practices of learning, teaching, supervising, and researching. *Harvard Educational Review, 72*(1), 67-92.

LaBoskey, V. K. (2004). The methodology of self-study and its theoretical underpinnings. In J. J. J. Loughran, M. L. Hamilton, V. K. LaBoskey, & T. Russell (Eds.), *International handbook of self-study of teaching and teacher education practices* (Vol. 1, pp. 817-869). Springer.

Lakoff, G. (1993). The contemporary theory of metaphor. In A. Ortony (Ed.), *Metaphor and thought* (pp. 202-250). Cambridge University Press.

Lakoff, G., & Johnson, M. (1980). *Metaphors we live by*. The University of Chicago Press.

Lakoff, G., & Johnson, M. (1999). *Philosophy in the flesh: The embodied mind and its challenge to Western thought*. Basic Books.

Lakoff, G., & Nunez, R. E. (2000). *Where mathematics comes from: How the embodied mind brings mathematics into being*. Basic Books.

Leithwood, K. (2010). Transformational school leadership. In E. Baker, B. McGaw, & P. Peterson (Eds.), *International encyclopedia of education* (3rd ed.). Elsevier.

Leithwood, K. (2012). *The Ontario leadership framework 2012*. Toronto, Canada: The Institute for Education Leadership.

Leithwood, K. (2013). Forward. In J. Brandon, P. Hanna, R. Morrow, K. Rhyason, & S. Schmold, (Eds.), *The Alberta framework for school system success* (pp. vii-ix). CASS.

Lessard, S., Caine, V., & Clandinin, D. J. (2015). A narrative inquiry into familial and school curriculum making: Attending to multiple worlds of Aboriginal youth and families. *Journal of Youth Studies*, *18*(2), 197-214.

Levi-Strauss, C. (1966). *The savage mind*. Free Press.

Little Bear, L. (2000). Jagged worldviews colliding. In M. Battiste (Ed.), *Reclaiming Indigenous voice and vision* (pp. 77-85). UBC Press.

Loughran, J., & Northfield, J. (1998). A framework for the development of self-study practice. In M. L. Hamilton (Ed.), *Reconceptualizing teaching practice: Self-study in teacher education* (pp. 7–18). Falmer Press.

Luthans, F., & Avolio, B. J. (2003). Authentic leadership development. *Positive organizational scholarship*, *241*, 258.

Lyle, E. (2017). Autoethnographic approaches to an identity conscious curriculum. In E. Lyle (Ed.), *At the intersection of selves and subject: Exploring the curricular landscape of identity* (pp. 1-8). Sense.

Lyons, N., & LaBoskey, V. K. (Eds.). (2002). *Narrative inquiry in practice: Advancing the knowledge of teaching*. Teachers College Press.

Lyotard, J. F. (1984). *The postmodern condition: A report on knowledge* (Vol. 10). U of Minnesota Press.

Madden, R. (2013). *Being ethnographic: A guide to the theory and practice of ethnography*. Sage.

Madison, S. D. (2012). *Critical ethnography: Methods, ethics, and performance* (2nd ed.). Sage.

Malinowski, B. (2013). *Argonauts of the Western Pacific: An account of native enterprise and adventure in the archipelagoes of Melanesian New Guinea*. Routledge (Original work published 1922).

Markides, J. (2017). Reconciling an ethical framework for living well in the world of research. In J. Markides & L. Forsythe (Eds.), *Looking back and living forward: Indigenous research rising up* (pp. 291-300). Brill Sense.

Markides, J. (2018). Being Indigenous in the Indigenous education classroom. In E. Lyle (Ed.), *Fostering a relational pedagogy: Self-study as transformative praxis* (pp. 35-44). Brill Sense.

Markides, D., & Miller, S. (2018). Sharing stories: Duoethnographically evoking mathematics teacher identities through narratives. In E. Lyle (Ed.), *The negotiated self: Employing reflexive inquiry to explore teacher identity* (pp. 149-161). Brill Sense.

Markides, J. & Markides, D. (2020). The conversation we never had: Shared autobiography in relation to place and each other. In E. Lyle (Ed.), *Identity landscapes: Contemplating place and the construction of self* (pp. 114-123). Brill Sense.

Marzano, R. J. (2007). *The art and science of teaching: A comprehensive framework for effective instruction*. ASDC.

Marzano, R. J., Frontier, T., & Livingston, D. (2011). *Effective supervision: Supporting the art and science of teaching*. ASCD.

Maturana, H. R., & Varela, F. J. (1987). *The tree of knowledge: The biological roots of human understanding*. New Science Library/Shambhala Publications.

McDiarmid, J. (2019). *Highway of tears: A true story of racism, indifference, and the pursuit of justice for missing and murdered indigenous women and girls*. Atria Books.

McLaren, P. (2001). Bricklayers and bricoleurs: A Marxist addendum. *Qualitative Inquiry, 7*(6), 700-705.

McLaren, P. (2015). *Life in schools: An introduction to critical pedagogy in the foundations of education*. Routledge.

Merriam, S. B. (2009). *Qualitative research: A guide to design and interpretation*. Jossey-Bass.

Mishler, E. (1990). Validation in inquiry-guided research: The role of exemplars in narrative studies. *Harvard educational review, 60*(4), 415-443.

Mooney, R. L. (1957). The researcher himself. *Research for curriculum improvement, Association for Supervision and Curriculum Development, 1957 yearbook* (pp. 154-186). Association for Supervision and Curriculum Development.

Morgan, G. (2006). *Images of organization*. Sage.

Morrison, K. (2008). Educational philosophy and the challenge of complexity theory. *Education Philosophy and Theory, 40*(1), 19-34.

Muhammad, A. (2009). *Transforming school culture: How to overcome staff division*. Solution Tree Press.

Munby, H. (1986). Metaphor in the thinking of teachers: An exploratory study. *Journal of Curriculum Studies, 18*(2), 197-209.

Naganga, L., & Kambutu, J. (2013). Michael Apple: A modern day critical pedagogue. In J. D. Kirylo (Ed.), *A critical pedagogy of resistance: 34 pedagogues we need to know* (pp. 1-4). Sense.

Nieto, S. (2006). *Teaching as political work: Learning from courageous and caring teachers*. The Longfollow Lecture. Sarah Lawerence College. Retrieved from https://eric.ed.gov/?id=ED497692

Nisbett, R. E. (2003). *The geography of thought: How Asians and Westerners think differently*. Free Press.

Noddings, N. (2004). War, critical thinking, and self-understanding. *Phi delta kappan, 85*(7), 488-495.

O'Reilly, K. (2012). *Ethnographic methods*. Routledge.

Ortony, A. (1993). Metaphor, language, and thought. In A. Ortony (Ed.), *Metaphor and thought* (pp. 1-16). Cambridge University Press.
Patterson, K. A. (2003). *Servant leadership: A theoretical model*. Regent University.
Pinar, W., & Grumet, M. R. (1976). *Toward a poor curriculum*. Kendall/Hunt Publishing Company.
Pinar, W. F. (2001). The researcher as bricoleur: The teacher as public intellectual. *Qualitative Inquiry, 7*(6), 696-700.
Pirie, S. E. B., & Keiren, T. E. (1994). Beyond metaphor: Formalising in mathematic understanding within constructivist environments. *For the Learning of Mathematics. 14*(1), 39-43.
PISA Worldwide Rankings. (2018). http://factsmaps.com/pisa-worldwide-ranking-average-score-of-math-science-reading/
Popham, W. J. (2013). Objectives. In D. J. Flinders, & S. J. Thornton (Eds.), *The curriculum studies reader* (4th ed., pp. 95-108). Routledge.
Pound, E. (1970). *Guide to kulchur* (Vol. 257). New Directions Publishing.
Principe, J., & Barnes, B. (2011). Architects [Song recorded by Rise Against]. On *Endgame*. Sony/ATV.
Province of Alberta. (2018). *School act*. Alberta Queen's Printer.
Quinn, D. (1999) *Beyond civilization: Humanity's next great adventure*. Random House.
Quinn, M. (Ed.). (2018a). *Complexifying curriculum studies: Reflections on the generative and generous gifts of William E. Doll, Jr*. Routledge.
Quinn, M. (2018b). Introduction—from "the echo of God's laughter". In M. Quinn (Ed.), *Complexifying curriculum studies: Reflections on the generative and generous gifts of William E. Doll Jr*. (pp. 1-15). Routledge.
Reeves, D. B. (2009). *Leading change in your school: How to conquer myths, build commitment, and get results*. ASCD.
Renert, M. (2011). Mathematics for life: Sustainable mathematics education. *For the Learning of Mathematics, 31*(1), 20-26.
Ridley, D. (2012). *The literature review: A step-by-step guide for students* (2nd ed.). Sage.
Robertson, J. S. (2013). Noam Chomsky: Father of modern linguistics. In J. D. Kirylo (Ed.), *A critical pedagogy of resistance: 34 pedagogues we need to know* (pp. 21-24). Sense.
Robinson, V. (2011). *Student-centered leadership*. Jossey-Bass.
Robinson, V., Lloyd, C., & Rowe, K. (2008). The impact of leadership on student outcomes: An analysis of the differential effects of leadership types. *Educational Administration Quarterly, 44*(5), 635–674.
Rogers, C. R. (1995). *On becoming a person: A therapist's view of psychotherapy*. Houghton Mifflin Harcourt
Rorty, R. (1979). *Philosophy and the mirror of nature*. Princeton University Press.
Rorty, R. (1984). Habermas and Lyotard on post-modernity. *Praxis International, 4*(1), 32-44.
Ross, R. (1996). *Returning to the teachings: Exploring Aboriginal justice*. Penguin.
Samaras, A. P. (2010). Explorations in using arts-based self-study methods. *International Journal of Qualitative Studies in Education, 23*(6), 719-736.
Samaras, A. P. (2011). *Self-study teacher research: Improving your practice through collaborative inquiry*. Sage.

Samaras, A. P., & Freese, A. R. (2006). *Self-study of teaching practices primer* (Vol. 12). Peter Lang.

Samaras, A. P., Hicks, M. A., & Garvey Berger, J. (2004). Self-study through personal history. In J. J. J. Loughran, M. L. Hamilton, V. K. LaBoskey, & T. Russell (Eds.), *International handbook of self-study of teaching and teacher education practices* (Vol. 1, pp. 905-942). Springer.

Sumara, D., & Davis, B. (2013). Interrupting heteronormativity: Towards a queer curriculum theory. In D. J. Flinders, & S. J. Thornton (Eds.), *The curriculum studies reader* (4th ed., pp. 315-329). Routledge.

Sumara, D., Davis, B., & Laidlaw, L. (2001). Canadian identity and curriculum theory: An ecological, postmodern perspective. *Canadian Journal of Education, 26*(2), 144-163.

Saul, J. R. (2014). *The comeback: How Aboriginals are reclaiming power and influence.* Viking Press.

Schneider, M., & Somers, M. (2006). Organizations as complex adaptive systems: Implications of complexity theory for leadership research. *The Leadership Quarterly, 17*(4), 351-365.

Schön, D. A. (1993). Generative metaphor: A perspective on problem-setting in social policy. In A. Ortony (Ed.), *Metaphor and thought* (pp. 137-163). Cambridge University Press.

Seashore Louis, K., Leithwood, K., Wahlstrom, K., & Anderson, S. (2010). *Investigating the links to improved student learning.* University of Minnesota.

Seidel, J. (2014). Losing wonder: Thoughts on nature, mortality, education. In J. Seidel & D.W. Jardine (Eds.), *Ecological pedagogy, Buddhist pedagogy, hermeneutic pedagogy: Curriculum for miracles* (pp. 133-152). Peter Lang.

Seidel, J., & Jardine, D. (2014). *Ecological pedagogy, Buddhist pedagogy, hermeneutic pedagogy: Curriculum for miracles.* Peter Lang.

Sensoy, O., & DiAngelo, R. (2012). *Is everyone really equal? An introduction to key concepts in social justice education.* Teachers College Press.

Sfard, A. (1994). Reification as birth of a metaphor. *For the Learning of Mathematics. 14*(1), 44-55.

Shields, C. M. (2016). *Transformative leadership primer.* Peter Lang.

Shor, I. (1992). *Empowering education: Critical teaching for social change.* Heinemann.

Smith, D, G. (1999). The hermeneutic imagination and the pedagogical text. In D, G, Smith (Ed.), *Pedagon: Human sciences, pedagogy and culture* (pp. 27-44). Peter Lang.

Smith, L. T. (1999/2012). *Decolonizing methodologies: Research and Indigenous peoples.* Zed Books.

Somerville, M. (2012). The critical power of place. In S. R. Steinberg & G. S. Cannella (Eds.), *Critical qualitative research reader* (pp. 67-81). Peter Lang.

Staudinger, U. M. (1999). Older and wiser? Integrating results on the relationship between age and wisdom-related performance. *International Journal of Behavioral Development, 23*(3), 641-664.

Steinberg, S. R. (2012a). Critical cultural studies research: Bricolage in action. In S. R. Steinberg & G. S. Cannella (Eds.), *Critical qualitative research reader* (pp. 182-197). Peter Lang.

Steinberg, S. R. (2012b). What's critical about qualitative research? In S. R. Steinberg & G. S. Cannella (Eds.), *Critical qualitative research reader* (p. ix). Peter Lang.

Steinberg, S. R., & Kincheloe, J. L. (2018). About power and critical pedagogy. In J. L. Kincheloe & S. R. Steinberg (Eds.), *Classroom teaching: An introduction* (2nd ed., pp. 29-43). Peter Lang.

Sumara, D. J., & Luce-Kapler, R. (1996). (Un) becoming a teacher: Negotiating identities while learning to teach. *Canadian Journal of Education/Revue canadienne de l'éducation,* 65-83.

Tarc, M. A. (2011). Curriculum as difficult inheritance. *Journal of Curriculum and Pedagogy*, 8(1), 17-19.

Thompson, E. (2010). *Mind in life*. Harvard University Press.

Tobin, K. (2009). Tuning into others' voices: Radical listening, learning from difference, and escaping oppression. *Cultural Studies of Science Education*, 4, 505-511.

Todd, S. (2003). Listening as an attentiveness to 'dense plots'. In *Learning from the other: Levinas, psychoanalysis, and ethical possibilities in education* (pp. 117-140). SUNY Press.

Tristán, J. M. B. (2013, February 6). Henry Giroux: The necessity of critical pedagogy in dark times. *Global Education Magazine*. https://truthout.org/articles/a-critical-interview-with-henry-giroux/

Tuck, E. (2009). Re-visioning Action: Participatory Action Research and Indigenous Theories of Change. *The Urban Review*, 41(1), 47-65. doi: 10.1007/s11256-008-0094-x

Varela, F. J., Thompson, E., & Rosch, E. (2016). *The embodied mind: Cognitive science and human experience*. MIT press.

Wadlington, E. (2013). John Dewey: Pragmatist, philosopher, and advocate of progressive education. In J. D. Kirylo (Ed.), *A critical pedagogy of resistance: 34 pedagogues we need to know* (pp. 29-32). Sense.

Wagamese, R. (2011a). *For Joshua: An Ojibway father teaches his son*. Anchor Canada.

Wagamese, R. (2011b). *One story, one song*. D & M Publishers.

Wagamese, R. (2011c). *A quality of light*. Doubleday Canada.

Wagamese, R. (2014). *Medicine walk*. McClelland & Stewart.

Wagamese, R. (2016). *Embers: One Ojibway's Meditations*. D & M Publishers.

Wagamese, R. (2019). *One Drum: Stories and ceremonies for a planet*. D & M Publishers.

Weaver, W. (1948). Science and complexity. *American Scientist*, 36(4), 536-544.

Weber, A. (2017). *Matter and desire: An erotic ecology*. Chelsea Green.

Weber, S. J., & Mitchell, C. (1995). *That's funny you don't look like a teacher: Interrogating images, identity, and popular culture*. Routledge.

Whitaker, T. (2013). *What great principals do differently: Eighteen things that matter most*. Routledge.

Whitehead, J. (2004). What counts as evidence in selfstudies of teacher education practices. In J. J. J. Loughran, M. L. Hamilton, V. K. LaBoskey, & T. Russell (Eds.), *International handbook of self-study of teaching and teacher education practices* (Vol. 1, pp. 871-904). Springer.

Wilson, S. (2008). *Research is ceremony: Indigenous research methods*. Fernwood Publishing.

Winchell, M., Kress, T. M., & Tobin, K. (2016). Teaching/learning radical listening: Joe's legacy among three generations of practitioners. In *Practicing critical pedagogy* (pp. 99-112). Springer, Cham.

Youngblood H. J. (2000). The context of the state of nature. In M. Battiste (Ed.), *Reclaiming Indigenous voice and vision* (pp. 11-38). UBC Press.

Zhang, H. (2018). Toward the reenchantment of curriculum: A study on William Doll's postmodern curriculum theory. In M. Quinn (Ed.), *Complexifying curriculum studies: Reflections on the generative and generous gifts of William E. Doll Jr.* (pp. 29-37). Routledge.

Counterpoints
PRIMERS
in Education

Counterpoints Primers are designed to provide a brief and concise introduction or supplement to specific topics in education. Although sophisticated in content, these primers are written in an accessible style, making them perfect for undergraduate and graduate classroom use. Each volume includes a glossary of key terms and a References and Resources section.

To order, please contact our Customer Service Department:
peterlang@presswarehouse.com (within the US)
orders@peterlang.com (outside the US)

To find out more about this and other Peter Lang book series, or to browse a full list of education titles, please visit our website:
www.peterlang.com

Published primers include:

- *Critical Pedagogy* (1st and 2nd editions) by Joe L. Kincheloe
- *Critical Constructivism* by Joe L. Kincheloe
- *Foucault and Education* by Gail McNicol Jardine
- *Literacy Primer* by Brett Elizabeth Blake & Robert W. Blake
- *Standards* by Raymond A. Horn, Jr.
- *Mentorship* by Carol A. Mullen
- *Piaget and Education* by David W. Jardine
- *Popular Culture* (1st and rev. editions) by John A. Weaver
- *Teaching Writing* by P.L. Thomas
- *John Dewey* by Douglas J. Simpson
- *No Child Left Behind* by Frederick M. Hess & Michael J. Petrilli

- *Self-Study of Teaching Practices* by Anastasia P. Samaras & Anne R. Freese
- *Authentic Assessment* by Valerie J. Janesick
- *Bakhtin* by Carolyn M. Shields
- *American Public Education Law* (1st, 2nd, and 3rd editions) by David C. Bloomfield
- *History of American Education* by David Boers
- *Standardized Testing* by Richard P. Phelps
- *Feminist Theories and Education* by Leila E. Villaverde
- *Studying Urban Youth Culture* by Greg Dimitriadis
- *Action Research* by Patricia H. Hinchey
- *Pedagogy* by Philip M. Anderson
- *Race and Education* by Aaron David Gresson III
- *Rethinking Technology in Schools* by Vanessa Elaine Domine
- *Social Theory in Education* by Philip Wexler
- *Aesthetics* by Boyd White
- *Vygotsky on Education* by Robert Lake
- *Peace and Pedagogy* by Molly Quinn
- *Transformative Leadership* by Carolyn M. Shields
- *History of American Higher Education* by Margaret Cain McCarthy
- *Charter School* by Anne Marie Tryjankowski
- *Civic Youth Work* by Ross Velure Roholt & Michael Baizerman
- *Arts-Based Research* by James Haywood Rolling, Jr.
- *Uncovering Black Heroes: Lesser-Known Stories of Liberty and Civil Rights* by David Boers
- *Enacting Self-Study: Learning and Leading Through Love* by Derek Markides

www.ingramcontent.com/pod-product-compliance
Ingram Content Group UK Ltd.
Pitfield, Milton Keynes, MK11 3LW, UK
UKHW021849210426
5322IPUK00022B/561